LEADERSHIP STYLES AND THEORIES IN INDIA AND ABROAD

LEADERSHIP STYLES AND THEORIES IN INDIA AND ABROAD

By
Ziauddin Khairoowala
Mohd. Ashraf Ali

ANMOL PUBLICATIONS PVT. LTD.
NEW DELHI - 110 002 (INDIA)

ANMOL PUBLICATIONS PVT. LTD.
H.O.: 4374/4B, Ansari Road, Daryaganj
New Delhi - 110 002
Ph.: 23261597, 23278000
B.O.: No. 1015, Ist Main Road, BSK III Stage
III Phase, III Block
Bangalore-560 085 (India)
Visit us at: www.anmolpublications.com

Leadership Styles and Theories in India and Abroad

First Published, 2006

ISBN 81-261-2647-7

PRINTED IN INDIA

Published by J.L. Kumar for Anmol Publications Pvt. Ltd., New Delhi - 110 002 and Printed at Mehra Offset Press, Delhi.

CONTENTS

ACKNOWLEDGEMENTS

Leadership is an important factor in any form of organization whether it is small or big. One of the most significant features of the leader situation is the style or behaviour of the leaders. It became a focal point in the emergence of modern human resources management in the organizational psychology. Many studies were undertaken on leadership styles adopted in bigger organizations. But relatively only a few attempts have been made to study the leadership styles adopted by owner-managers as leaders in Small Scale Industries. A study of this feature is necessary to understand the leadership in its total as many of the Small Scale Industries are being managed by owner managers themselves. The present study of "Leadership styles and theories in India and Abroad" is an attempt in this direction.

We are grateful to Mr. Naseem Ahmad, Vice-Chancellor, A.M.U., Aligarh for his moral support in completing this work.

We sincerely express our deep sense of gratitude to Prof. M. Mushtaque Ahmed, Dean and Chairman, Department of Commerce, A.M.U., Aligarh, who has been a constant source of inspiration and encouragement to us during the course of this study.

We are thankful to Prof. Samiuddin and Prof. Mahfoozur Rahman, Prof. Nafees Baig, Prof. A. Farooq Khan, Prof. Qamaruddin Khan, Prof. Sharifur Rehman, Prof. Badar Alam Iqbal, Prof. Mohammad Ali, Prof. Shaikh Mastan, Prof. Saleem

Uddin, Dr. Naimuddin Siddiqui, Dr. Javed Alam Khan, Dr. Sibqhatullah Farooqui, Dr. S. M. Imamul Haque, Dr. S. Husain Ashraf, Dr. A.Q. Khan, Dr. Imran Siddiqui, Dr. M. Mohsin Khan, Dr. Imran Saleem, Dr. Nawab Ali, Dr. Nasir Zameer Qureshi, Mrs. Sheeba Hamid, Mr. Mohd Shamim, Dr. Nafees A. Khan, Dr. Mohd Asif Khan, Dr. Mohd Yameen, A.M.U., Aligarh, for their moral and academic encouragement in completing this work.

Our special thanks goes to Dr. Mulat Demeke, Dean, Faculty of Business and Economics (FBE), Addis Ababa University (A.A.U.) Ethiopia, Ato Tsegabrhan, Mekonen, Associate Dean, FBE, A.A.U., Addis Ababa, Ato Meseret, Chairman, Department of Management, A.A.U., Ato Mohd Seid, Ex. Chairman., Department of Management, A.A.U., Addis Ababa. Dr. Zewdie Shibre Ex. Dean, Dr. Mehret, Ato Teshome, Ato Mulugeta, Ato Buzuwork, Ato Jamal, Dr. Salehu Anteneh, Dr. Tilahun, Dr. Thadese, Prof. K. Rajeshwar Rao, Prof. G. Krishna Murty, Dr. Gurmeet Singh, Mr. Laxmikant, Departments of Management and Accounting, A.A.U., Addis Ababa, Ethiopia.

We are also grateful to Prof. V. Surendar, Dean, Faculty of Commerce, Osmania University, Hyderabad, Prof. B.R. Ananthan, Department of Management, Mysore University, Mysore, Prof. C. Suryanarayana, Department of Commerce and Business Management, Andhra University, Prof. G. Prasad, Department of Commerce and Business Management, Nagarjuna University, Guntur., Prof. H. Venkateshwarlu, Prof. K.V. Achlapathy, Department of Commerce, Osmania University, Hyderabad, Prof. K. Krishna Reddy, Head, Department of Commerce, Kakatiya University, Warangal, Prof. R.K. Mishra, Chairman, Finance Division, Institute of Public Enterprise, O.U. Campus, Hyderabad. Prof. G.C. Aggarwal, Allahabad, Prof. M.N. Ansari, Department of Commerce, B.H.U., Banaras, Prof. Nisar Ahmad, J.M.I., New

Delhi, Prof. A.A. Ansari, Head, Department of Commerce, J.M.I., New Delhi for their encouragement during the course of writing this book.

In writing this book, we have drawn upon the authorities on this subject and have acknowledged them at their proper places. Any lapses in acknowledgement are not deliberate and are likely to be due to oversight.

We thankful M/s Anmol Publications Pvt. Ltd., New Delhi and its staff in bringing out this volume within a very short period of time, so perfectly in a good shape.

Last but not the least we would like to mention about the tremendous forbearance shown by our family members Mr. Hanif Uddin Khairoowala, Mrs. Shamim Hanif, Mrs. Rani Firdaus, Mohiuddin Khairoowala, Miss. Naghma Zia, Miss Bushra Zia, Mohd. Mohsin and Mohd. Wasim, M. Khader Ali, Mumtaaz, Farzana Ali during the years of study, which enabled us to complete this book.

Dr. Ziauddin Khairoowala

Dr. Mohd. Ashraf Ali

1

INTRODUCTION

Human beings are the most precious part of civilization as well as of organization without leadership, an organization is only a confusion of people and machines. 'Leadership' is the ability to persuade others to seek defined objectives enthusiastically. It is the human factor that binds a group together and motivates it towards goals. The leader's act of motivation is similar in effect to that of the secret chemical that turns the insect pupa into a butterfly with all the beauty that was the pupa's potential. Leadership transforms potential organization and its people into reality.[1]

The leaders who work with in the organization, are governed by certain factors, forces acting on the manager, forces acting on the subordinates, forces acting on the situation. In any given situation, the behaviour of the manager is influenced by his own personality; that is, leadership is perceived on the basis of his background, knowledge and experience. The important forces affecting him arc: His value system; that is, the relative importance he attaches to organizational efficiency, the personal growth of his subordinates, and company profits. His confidence in his subordinates, which is influenced by the knowledge and competence they have. His own leadership inclination; that is whether he can function comfortably and naturally or whether he is uncomfortable when operating in a team.

The type of organization for which he works, its values and traditions which are communicated through job description, policy announcements and public statements by top executives. The size of a working unit, its geographical location, and the extent of inter-and intra-organizational security which is needed to attain company goals. That ultimately affect the quality and extent of employee participation. Cohesiveness, permissiveness, mutual acceptance and a common purpose also influence the functioning of a group. The nature of the problem itself may determine whether authority should be delegated to subordinates, and, if so, to what extent.

There are enormous and different theories of leadership, which were developed by different authors. There were a number of differences among these theories. This has been largely because leadership discusses about the personality and behaviour of people and the different external and situational factors that surround the leader.

Statement of Problem

There is a growing awareness towards professionalizing the management of large scale industries where every major activity has been brought under the care of a professional manager. The contributors to the capital now have shifted their role of managing the enterprise to the professionals. Hence, the success of the industry is to a greater extent dependent on the ability of the managers to manage the activities in a scientific and systematic manner.

Bigger industries can afford to hire the services of professionals whereas the small industries could not do so because their economies do not permit them to employ professionals who are to be paid huge sums of salaries and, therefore, the small entrepreneurs must naturally combine in themselves the qualities of professional manager to run the industry successfully. As professional management is a question of greater learning and wide experience, unless and until these are ensured in respect of small industries there can not be a definite success.

There is a growing tendency of small scale industries entering into sickness. The reasons may be numerous. But the vital reason may be cited to that of the absence of the services of a professional leader. Most of the industry failures can be attributed to that of leadership failure leader, as a manager, must have the capability to adopt style/styles according to the situation. Usually the small scale industries are started hastily in order to take advantage of the concessions offered by the Government. The entrepreneurs are not sure whether they combine in themselves the important quality of managing i.e., leading. Thus, those entrepreneurs who could lead their industry on scientific lines flourished and others are entering into sickness.

Generally, the small industrialists manage their units in the traditional way and hence the production, personnel, marketing and finance are not separate subjects for them. The managers of small scale Industries are not being supported by the services of technical specialists and functional people as in the case of large units. In dealing with the problems the many of the managers/owners of SSI take decision themselves and determine the prosperity of these units. Therefore, the decision-making style of owner-managers on overall problems directly or indirectly influences the health of the organization. It is can be added that it has been debated in various seminars and conferences whether finance or personnel problems or marketing problems are responsible for this failure. One view is that may be finance or personnel problems or even marketing, all these problems come under the functions of leadership. Therefore, leadership plays a dominant role in placing the units in success or failure which is also true in case of small scale industries.

Review of Literature

In the following paragraphs some of the studies on leadership have been reviewed.

The initial and original studies on leadership were carried out at the university of Iowa by Lewin, Lippitt and White (1939).[2] They focused on the decision-making component of the leader's behaviour and classified leaders into three different styles viz; Authoritarian, Democratic and Laissez-Faire. They were tested on high school children.

Bales (1950)[3] and Hare etal. (1955)[4] have conducted work a study of small group. They found that in small group two different kinds of leaders where emerged. One was the task-leader characterized by those who talk more and who offer suggestions and the other was called socio-emotional leader represented by those who make it easier for others to talk and offer psychological support.

Researchers of Survey Research Centre at the University of Michigan Katz (1950)[5], Mann & Dent (1954)[6] and Morse & Reimer (1956)[7] observed that general supervision and supervisors who were employee-oriented tend to associate with producing groups and those supervisors who were job-oriented resulted in high levels of productivity. A similar study was undertaken by Weissenberg and Kavanaugh (1972)[8] who argued that the two dimensions are independent of one other.

One of the most widely read articles on leadership was written in 1958 by Robert Tannenbaum and Warren H. Schmidt.[9] In this article, leadership was considered to represent a range of behaviour. Their approach contrasts the use of authority by the boss versus the amount of freedom provided to subordinates. Seven styles of leadership are presented by the study viz., (i) Manager makes decisions and announces it; (ii) Manager 'Sells' decision; (iii) Manager presents ideas and invites questions; (iv) Manager presents tentative decision subject to change; (v) Manager presents problem, gets suggestions, makes decision; (vi) Manager defines limits, asks group to make decision, and (vii) Manager permits subordinates to function within the limits defined by supervisor. This article suggested that leadership consists of three sets of forces; those in the manager, in subordinates and in the situations and also concluded that the successful leader is one who can assess the forces and determines appropriate leadership action at any given time.

Stogdill and Coons (1957)[10] have tentatively identified nine dimensions of the nine only two dimensions namely initiating structure and consideration structure. The first one refers to structuring of role of one's self and that of others while the second refers to cordial relationship with persons.

Douglas McGregor (1960)[11] has pointed out in his book entitled *"The Human Side of Enterprise"* that there are at least four variables involved in leadership. They are (i) The characteristics of the leader; (ii) The attitudes, needs and other personal characteristics of the followers; (iii) The characteristics of the organization such as its purpose, its structure and nature of the task to be performed; and (iv) The social, economic and political milieu. Also he noted that "Leadership is not a property of the individual, but a complex relationship among these variables". He identified (1967)[12] two major perpetual structures which were labeled as theory X for authoritarian approach and theory Y for the participative approach.

A theory of effective management known as "Managerial Grid" was advocated by Blake and Mouton (1964).[13] They identified two dimensions of effective leadership one was concern for people and the other was with the production.

Victor H. Vroom (1973)[14] was one of the researcher who

propounded the Expectancy Theories of Motivation. He proposed the theory of leadership with the help of W. Yetton.

Fiedler (1964)[15] developed a model for leadership effectiveness from the basic proposition that the most effective behaviour for leaders to engage is contingent upon characteristics of the situation. According to him, any managerial situation in an organization can be classified on the basis of the extent to which the situation is favourable to the leader. He used two-factor approach to leadership style or the 'relationship oriented' leader. The group situation is dominated by three factors listed in order of importance: Leader-member relations, Task-structure and Leader-position power.[16]

The results of a recent comprehensive review and analysis of research on Fiedler model done by Strube and Gracia (1981)[17] proved a high degree of over all support for the theory while Garaen et.al (1970)[18] and failed to support the model.

One of the theories of leadership that has received major recent interest is an outgrowth of expectancy theorites of motivation. Robert J. House[19] and others view the leader's primary role attempting to have a favourable impact on subordinate's motivation. Four kinds of leadership behaviour are identified, viz., (i) directive, (ii) supportive, (iii) participative and (iv) achievement oriented.

Gordon[20] has summarized his research on leadership which includes the studies of the authoritarian leader, the emergent or natural leader, and formal leaders in bureaucratic organizations he also covered the problem of training leaders.

Apple White[21] has studied the leadership roles and functions and found that leaders lead in three conditions i.e. the relationship of communication to leadership, the problem of leader assessment and the concept of leadership styles.

Albert S. King[22] uses a developmental perspective to create an evolutionary tree of leadership theory. He identified nine evolutionary eras with other researchers in each Era focusing a specific theme of leadership. He also discus the requirements of the tenth Era-The Integrative Era-which hopefully will bring together different theory of leadership. This is shown in the form of diagram below:

FIGURE

The Evolutionary Tree of Leadership Theory

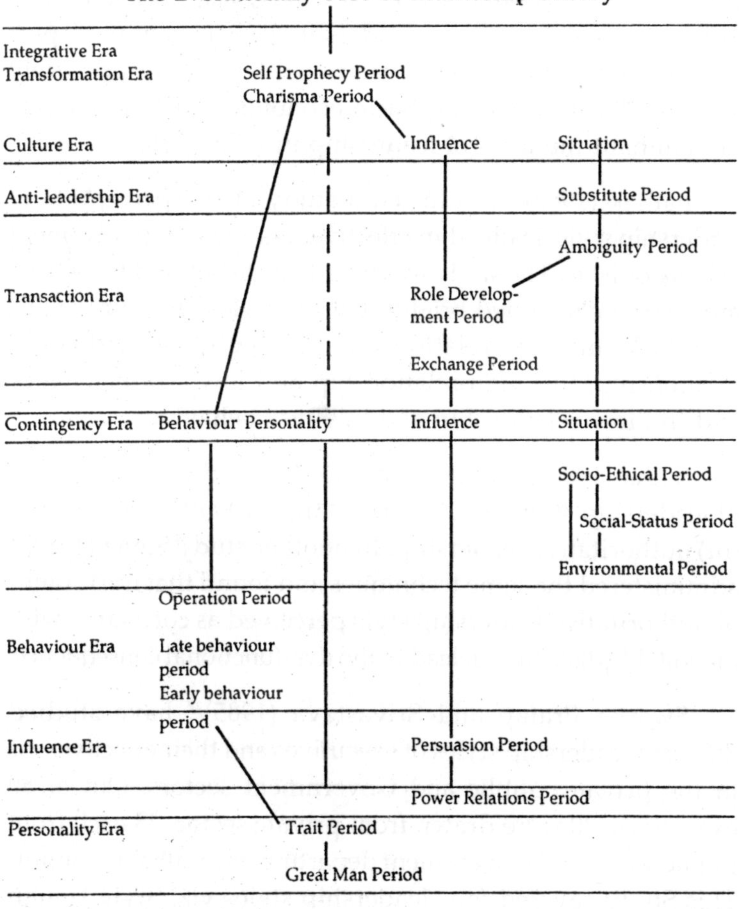

Lokhande and S.N. Singh's (1977)[23] study covered five leadership patterns viz., (i) Traditional leadership, (ii) political leadership, (iii) opinion-making leadership, (iv) Decision making leadership and (v) Caste leadership. The field investigation was carried out in the Community Development Block, Kanjhawala in the Union Territory of Delhi which is predominantly a rural area close to the city of Delhi. The study brings out the fact that there have been very poor growth and development of leadership in the villages under study. Socio-economic status, however, has been found to influence considerably the leadership structure with respect to extension programmes. Traditional leadership positively associated with caste and Socio-economic status still seems to dominant the form of leadership in village life.

Pathak (1980)[24] conducted a study of self-perception of leadership style, leadership effectiveness and job-involvement of bank officers. The study was based on Hersey and Blanchard model and concluded briefly that the styles are four viz., (i) high-task and low-relationship, (ii) high-task and high-relationship; (iii) high-relationship and low-task behaviour and (iv) low-relationship and low-task behaviour.

Sinha (1980)[25] in his study briefly listed out three types of leadership styles as (i) participative, (ii) authoritarian and (iii) authoritative leadership. In another study Sinha (1983)[26] administered the same techniques and found that nurturance or authoritative leadership style perceived as correlated with inequitable distribution lead to the dys-functional consequence.

Swarna Pratap and Srivastava (1985)[27] have studied different leadership styles of executives and their effectiveness in the private, public and Government sectors. Out of 80 executives, 30 were drawn from private sector, 25 each from public sector and Government departments located in Kanpur. This Study covered four leadership styles viz, **Style 1:** high task-low relationship (telling); **Style 2 :** high task-high relationship (selling); **Style 3:** low task-low relationship (delegating). The study states that not much difference in leadership effectiveness and style across different type of organizations is seen. High task-high relationship style i.e., **Style 2** was found to be predominant among executives of organizations. Results on style 1 (high task-low relationship) and style 3 (low-high relationship) show that the Indian executives do think on the lines of 'Concern for the People' but many of them still like to be benevolent autocrats rather than participative managers. The positive correlation of style 3 with its effectiveness dimension makes it obvious that efforts in the direction of participation may be successful.

Mutaya and Vijaykumar (1985)[28] by taking a sample of 68 Scientific personnel belonging to different research institutions under the ICAR conducted a study wherein they identified and described the styles under five headings viz., (i) Direction style, (ii) Negotiation style (iii) Consultative style (iv) Participative style and (v) Delegation style. They found that the predominant styles 'direction' followed by 'Delegation' and 'Participation'.

Remakanth (1986)[29] has undertaken a comparative study of Indian managers among different regions, religions, kinds of organizations etc., to examine the attitudes of managers with respect to success.

In another study Neelam Varma (1986)[30] made an attempt to examine the relative validity of the implicit leadership position by testing two groups of subjects (experienced i.e., executives and inexperienced i.e. students) on leadership dimension through a study conducted in Oil Refinery. The study suggests that people should be highly devoted to their work because it is the rare commodity in Indian conditions which helps to establish the viability of the naturant concept.

Singh and Janak Pandey (1986)[31] conducted a study on a sample of 250 respondents comprising of 150 workers, 50 supervisors and 50 line managers of an electric equipment manufacturing large public undertaking located in Northern India with the objective of showing the pattern of relationship between three leadership styles (i.e. participative, authoritarian and authoritative) with a different strategies of control, need satisfaction and commitment with the organization. In addition, it was also planned to study the differential effects of hierarchy and production versus service sections of the organization on perception of leadership styles, control mechanism, need satisfaction and commitment. The study brings out that participative and authoritative are positive styles of leadership. Authoritative may substitute participative till conditions in and organization do not permit but there is nothing very critical to suggest that the participative style of leadership would not work till there is a change in socio-cultural milieu of the Indian organizations. Another important finding of the studies is that the failure in introducing participative style of leadership is caused due to the inner compulsions, intrigues and interests of the proprietors which may be the State or the individuals. Probably this could not be attributed to the cultural ethos of the society.

Prabakar Singh (1987)[32] has undertaken a study on executives of an ineffective and effective organizations engaged in producing the same commodity. 200 respondents drawn randomly (110 executives from each organization) from these companies were sent the questionnaire. 75 of the ineffective and 69 of the effective organizations' executives returned filled in questionnaires. The Important finding of this study is that the nurturant-task leadership is the best leader behaviour for supervising the workmen and participative-task leadership is the best leader behaviour. In addition the study indicates that the organization, its objectives, culture and values shall to a large extent decide the type of leader behaviour.

Based on an extensive research on the subject, Rastogi (1987)[33] in his study points out that a leader should look at the organization as an evolutionary process towards desired future. He elaborates the essence of leadership as consisting of the following:

Creating a vision of the future, setting an example, reinforming desired behaviour and creating the ideal self-image. Empathy and Charisma are the two qualities that a leader needs.

The study conducted by the Venkatapathy (1990)[34] concludes that three leadership styles will be in the public and private sectors viz., benevolent, critical and development.

Scope of Study

Many studies were undertaken on leadership styles in large organizations. But relatively only a few attempts have been made to study the leadership styles in small scale industries. A study of this nature is a necessity to understand the leadership styles in small scale industries are being practiced by owner-managers.

Many people believe that there exists a difference between the concept of manager and leader. But many argue that both are synonymous. Theoretically, manager and leader may be distinguished. Thus, it is pertinent to mention here that effective manager requires effective leadership. However, as Mescon et al., (1973)[35] pointed out "a survey of the management literature discloses a general confusion concerning the role of the manager as opposed to that of the leader. An attempt to understand the nature of the manager's place in organization and enterprise becomes still more confused when the concept of the entrepreneur is introduced into the situation. The present trend towards solving this problem by using the terms leader, manager and entrepreneur interchangeably is no solution".

Leader, Manager and Entrepreneur Differentiated

These three classes of people differ in their orientation, sources of authority and types of interactions and their emphasis on goals sought in an organization. The manager is more institutionally oriented than the leader who is oriented towards group of individuals. The manager derives his authority from his formal position whereas for the leader the authority is sanctioned by the group. The types of interactions that the manager has are through formal lines but for the leader the interactions are through informal lines. The Paramount activity for a manager is attainment of organizational goals where as it is the attainment of the group goals which is very essential for the leader. The entrepreneur in the small scale industries is also in the position of a manager. He is also having a fewer number of employees under his control and hence he is curiously in a position of being at once an entrepreneur-manager-leader. This coincidence might help to a greater extent to understand the concept of leadership. Thus, this study envisages to examine the leadership styles of owner-managers in selected small scale industries of Nellore town.

Objectives

The specific objectives of the study are follows:

1. To review the concepts of leadership,
2. To review the theories of leadership.
3. To review the styles of leadership
4. To examine whether there is any relationship between the demographic variables such as age, education, experience and family background and attitudes of owner-managers, (leader)
5. To study empirically the various leadership styles adopted by owner-managers in small scale industries.

6. To Critically examine how for the age, education, experience and family background will influence the leadership styles of owner-manager.
7. To identify the problems and suggest suitable measures for the improvement of leadership styles in small scale industries.

Hypothesis

In the light of the above noted objectives, the following hypotheses have been formulated and tested:

1. There is correlation between the demographic variables such as age, education, experience and family background and attitudes of owner-managers.
2. Owner-managers use different types of leadership styles depending on different situations.
3. Leadership styles of owner-managers will vary with the type of decision, education, age, experience and family background.

Research Design

The design of the present study is based on "situational or contingency" view of leadership. Contingency theories of leadership have appeared over the past few years largely as a result of recognition of the fact that there is no single universal "best" leadership style. As their label implies, contingency theories of leadership are derived from the basic proposition that the most effective behaviour for leaders to engage in is contingent upon characteristics of the situation in which the leaders find themselves. [36] The contingency approach in leadership theory follows from the lack of consistent evidence as to the 'best leadership style' where style refers to behaviour that a person (i.e., the leader) exhibits when attempting to influence the activities of others as perceived by those others.[37]

The contingency model states that the most appropriate style of leadership depends on the situation in which the leader works. More specifically, the best leadership style depends on whether the situation is favourable, unfavourable or in an intermediate range of favorability to the leader. As the situation varies, leadership requirements vary.[38] In contingency theory there are, a large number of potential contingency variables and in Practice it is likely that a few will account of the major portion of the observed variance of behaviour.

The leader's ability and personal characteristics obviously influence and constrain what the leader does and how he or she behaves towards subordinates.[39] Thus, a number of personal, organizational and situational constraints may influence the actions of leader and those of the members belonging to his group. These may be categorized into two groups. They are:

1. Demographic -characteristics of owner-manager like age, education, family background, experience and attitudes.
2. Situational variables like nature of the decision and level of organization and such other structural and ecological variables.

Basic Variables of the Study

The basic variables that are being used for the present study are:-

1. **Independent variables:** Demographic characteristics of owner-managers like age, education, experience and family background in the organization.

2. **Situational Variables :** Referred to the contents of the decision. Seventeen different situations are comprised in this variable. They are:

Decision Relating to Production

(i) Decision relating to volume of output.

(ii) Decision relating to size, location and layout of plant.

(iii) Decision relating to Methods of Production

(iv) Decision relating to purchasing practices and the Amount of inventory.

(v) Decision relating to the methods of wage payment.

Decisions Concerned with Technical Matters

(vi) Decision to change the operating procedure.

(vii) Decision to purchase new equipment.

(viii) Decision to hire machinery.

(ix) Decision to employ new subordinates to operate the machine.

Decisions Concerned with Financial Matters

(x) Decision to purchase a new machine.

(xi) Decision to get a loan.

(xii) Decision to any other financial matter.

Decisions Concerned with Personnel Matters

(xiii) Decision to promote or punish the workers.

(xiv) Decision to take disciplinary action against employees.

(xv) Decision to assign a different job to workers.

(xvi) Decision to remove the workers.

(xvii) Decision to pay any compensation.

Sample Design and Data Base

Nellore district is one of the 23 districts of Andhra Pradesh which is one of the foremost States of the Indian Union accounting for 8.6 percent area and 7.8 percent of population. There are 93 municipalities in Andhra Pradesh out of which 3 are in Nellore District. The three Municipalities are Nellore, kavali and Gudur.

Nellore town is purposively selected for the present study because of considerations of proximity and familiarity. It happens to be the head quarters of Nellore district and `A' Grade Municipality. Though it is the fastest growing town in Andhra Pradesh, its industrial base is very thin and is essentially a commercial centre and is therefore typical of most urban centres in the country.

There are more than 2528 registered Small Scale Industries operating in Nellore district by the end of March 1990 out of which 602 are in Nellore town. With regard to unregistered units, the number is anybody's guess. Out of the registered small scale industries operating in Nellore town, sixty units are selected 'for the present study. They are selected neither randomly nor stratified according to the functions and products produced by the units because of some practical constraints. Therefore, units are selected conveniently according to their availability and date have been collected from those individuals who are willing to cooperate in the study.

Data have been gathered by administering a structured schedule to owner-mangers. Besides, personal interview has also been held with the respondents so as to get accurate information. Before proceeding to fill the schedule the researcher has made all efforts in explaining the poi ts wherever the respondent feels difficult to understand

The administered schedule to owner-manage consists of two sections. They are :

Section I : Deals with various questions regarding personal data of the respondents.

Section II : This section is the heart of the present study, emphasis being on the decision making style of owner-managers in their organizations.

Analytical Procedure

The data drawn from various sources have been subjected to well known statistical techniques like weighted mean, standard deviation and co-efficient of variation to compare the variability in the attitudes of owner-manager towards classical and modern approaches of leadership. In addition to the above, co-efficient of correlation and student 't' test by using Fisher's Z transformation formula have been extensively used so as to analyse the leadership styles.

Limitations of the Study

The study has been confined to sixty owner-managers owning small sĉale industries in Nelore town (A small industry, for the purpose, has been taken as the industry in which a capital below Rs. 35 Lakhs is invested in plant and machinery and Rs. 45 Lakhs in ancillary units). Every data gathering device has potentially biased and has specific to it certain validity threats. The same design framed and research method employed for the purpose of this study also has its limitations. They are :

1. The sample units of the study have been selected neither randomly nor stratified according to the functions and products produced by the units because of practical difficulties. Units have been selected conveniently according to their availability and data is collected from individuals who are willing to cooperate in the study.

2. Owing to financial constraints and time limit, the study has been restricted to only sixty owner-managers in the Mellore town.
3. Through the leadership is interpersonal relationship between the leader/manager and followers, the study is focused on the former only.
4. As the area of marketing is un-organised and complicated, it is deliberately left out from the study of decision making.
5. Managing Partner of the partnership firms is considered only as the owner-manager and distinction is not observed between the sole trading concerns and partnership firms.

Chapter Scheme

This study is divided into Eight Chapters. The First Chapter deals with introduction and review of a selective literature. The Second Chapter is devoted to Leadership-A Conceptual Approach. The Third Chapter deals with Theories of Leadership. The major concept which is required for clear comprehensive of the study of leadership styles is explained in the Fourth Chapter. The Fifth Chapter deals with the Personal Background of leaders. Leadership styles ado ted by the sample owner-managers are empirically found out n Chapter Six. The Seventh Chapter explains a practice of leadership theory in EEPC Ethiopia. The last Chapter is devoted to the presentation of Summary, Findings and Conclusions.

REFERENCES

1. H. Russell Johnston., *A New Conceptualization of Sources of Organizational Climate*, Addition-Wesley Publishing Company, 1977, pp. 95-103.
2. Lewin, K., Lippit, R., & White R., & White, R.K., Patterns of Aggressive Behaviour in Experimentally created, 'Social Climates', *Journal of Psychology*, 1939, pp. 271-299.

3. Bales, R.F., *Interaction Process Analysis: A Method for the Study of Small Groups*, Cambridge, 1950.
4. Hare, A.P., Borgatta, E.E., I & Bales, R.F., *Small Groups Studies in Social Group Interaction*, New York, 1955.
5. Katz, D., *Productivity, Supervision and Morale Among Rail-Road Workers*, An Arbor, Michigan, Institute for Social Research, 1950.
6. Mann, F.C., & Dent, J., The Supervisor Member of Two Organizational Families, *Harvard Business Review*, 32 (6), 1954, pp. 103-112.
7. Morse, N.C., & Remier, E., The Experimental change of two organizational variables, *Journal of Abnormal and Social Psychology*, 52, 1956, pp. 120-129.
8. Weissenburg, D., and Kavanaugh, M.H., "The Independence of Initiating and Structure and Consideration, A Review of Evidence," *Personal Psychology*, 25, 1972, pp. 119-130.
9. Tannenbaum, Robert and Warren, H. Schmidt, How to choose A Leadership Pattern, *Harvard Business Review*, March-April, 1958, pp. 95-101.
10. Stogdill, R.M., & Conns, A.E., (eds) *Leader Behaviour: Its Prescription and Measurement*, Columbus, Bureau of Business Research, Ohio-State University, 1957.
11. McGregor, Douglas, *The Human Side of Enterprises*, McGraw-Hill Book Company, New York, 1960, p. 182.
12. McGregor, Douglas, *The Professional Manager*, McGraw-Hill Book Company, New York, 1967. p. 58.
13. Blake Robert, R., *Managerial Grid*, Gulf Publishing Company, Texas, 1964, pp. 8-9.
14. Vroom, V.H., and Yetton, P.W., *Leadership and Decision Making*, Pittsburgh; University of Pittsburgh Press, 1973.
15. Fiedler, F.E., A Contingency Model of Leadership Effectiveness, Berkowitz (ed.) *Advances in Experimental Social Psychology*, Academic Press, New York, 1964.
16. Fiedler, F.E., *A Theory of Leadership Effectiveness*, McGraw-Hill Book Company, New York, 1967, p. 247.
17. Strube, M.J., and Garcia, J.E., Meta Analytic Investigation of Fiedler's Contingency Model of Leadership Effectiveness, *Psychological Bulletin*, 1981, p. 307-321.
18. Garaen G., Alvares, K.M., Orris, J.B., & Martella, J.A.,

Contingency Model of Leadership Effectivness, Antecedent Evidential Results, *Psychological Bulletin*, 1970.

19. House Robert, J., A Path Goal of Leadership Effectiveness, *Administrative Science Quarterly*, Volume 16, 1971, pp. 3212-340.
20. Gordon, T., *Group Centered Leadership*, Boston, Houghton Mifflin company, 1955, pp. 46-51.
21. Apple, W., Philip. B., *Organization Behaviour*, Englewood Cliffs, N.J. Prentice-Hall, Chapter 6, 1965.
22. Albert S. King, Evolution of Leadership Theory, *Vikalpa*, Volume, 15, No. 2 April-June, 1990, pp. 43-51.
23. Lokhande, M.R., and Singh, S.N., Leadership Patters and Social Change, *Journal of the Council of Social Development*, Volume, 7, No. 1 March, 1977, pp. 14-19.
24. Pathak, R.D., A Study of Self-Perception of Leadership Styles, Leadership Effectiveness and Job-Involvement of Bank Officers, *Prajna*, reprinted from Volume IX, 1980.
25. Sinha, J.B.P. *The Nuturant Task-Behaviour*, Concept Publishing Company, New Delhi, 1980.
26. Sinha, J.B.P., Socio-Technological Determinants of Work Values: A proposal Mimeograph, 1983, as quoted by Sinha R.P. & Jank in *Indian Journal of Industrial Relations*, 1986.
27. Swarna Pratap and Sirvatsava, S.K., Leadership Styles and Effectiveness - A Comparative Study , *Indian Journal of Industrial Relations*, Volume 21, No. 1 July, 1985, pp. 94-97.
28. Muttaya, B.C., and Vijay Kumar, S. , Leadership Styles, Perceived Need Satisfaction and subjective job Characteristics among scientific personnel, *Indian Journal of Industrial Relations*, Volume 21, No. 2, Oct, 1985, pp. 173-182.
29. Ramakanth. J., "Attitudes of Managers in public Enterprises," *Indian Journal of Industrial Relations*, Volume 21 No. 4, April, 986, pp. 39-404.
30. Neelam Verma, A Test of Implicit Personality Theories of Leadership, *Indian Journal of Industrial Relations*, Volume 22, No. 2, October, 1986, pp. 190-1999.
31. Singh, R.R. and Janak Pandey., Leadership Styles—Control, Strategies and Personal Consequence, *Indian Journal of Industrial Relations*, Volume 22, No. 1, July, 1986, pp. 41-51.
32. Prabakar Singh, Nurturan Task and Participative task leadership: The effective leader behaviours for Indian Industries,

Indian Journal of Industrial Relations, Volume 23 no. 2, October, 1987, pp. 197-202.

33. Rastogi, P.N., Essence of leadership, *Vikalpa*, Volume 12, No. 4, Oct.-Dec. 1987, p. 37.

34. Ventakapathy, Perception of Top management leadership styles and climate; A study of public and private executors, *Indian Journal of Industrial Relations*, Volume 25, No. 3, Jan, 1990 pp. 303-307.

35. Mescon, M.H., Hammond, W.R., Byars, L.L., & Forest, J.R., The Management and Enterprise, Macmillion, New York, 1973.

36. Danial, C., etal. "Managing Individual and Group Behaviour in Organisations", 1st edition, McGraw-Hill International Book Company, Japan, 1983, p. 307

37. Paul Hersey and Blanchard, K.H. *Management of Organizational Behaviour*, 4th edition, Prentice-Hall of India, Private Ltd., New Delhi, 1981, p. 139.

38. Davis, Keith, *Human Behaviour at Work: Organizational* Behaviour

2

LEADERSHIP: A CONCEPTUAL APPROACH

Leadership is a nomenclature given to quality of leader to lead. Quality of leading is one of the essential qualities, a manager is supposed to possess, because without leading, the activities of any enterprise may come to stand still. Quality of leadership is neither in born nor a God gifted. Any person, determined to acquire this quality, can do it by developing the skills of leading. A person, who leads, naturally established certain relationship between himself and his followers-subordinates in organization. Therefore, the term "leadership" is a result of relationship between a superior and subordinate which triggers a person's will to do and transform lukewarm desire for achievements into burning passions for successful accomplishment. The term "leadership" can be studied from two points of view- (i) Leadership as a quality and (ii) Leadership as a function.

Study of leadership as a quality involves the study of extent of capabilities to lead people. It more or less related to psychological, social and mental aspects that are required to acquire such a quality. Study of leadership as a function involves the study of activities to be undertaken be a leader i.e. the manager.

What leadership qualities do these small scale industrialists have? The basic leadership styles they adopt? The relation of their success or failure to the styles they adopt? Still remains to be an unexplored area by any researcher. Therefore, the importance of this study lies. No one has been able to measure precisely how important leadership is for the accomplishment of group and organizational goals. Conflicting views are found on these basic issue in the published literature. This study is also not an exception.

Without leadership an organization is only a confusion of people and machines. Leadership is the ability to persuade others to seek defined objectives enthusiastically. It transforms potential into reality. Leadership is replete with multi-myriad reams of research theories and multifarious definitions. After over fifty years of empirical investigation, leadership remains an enigma. It is wrapped up in a paper of management and is tightly knotted with the cords of incomprehension and confusion.

Stogdill (1974)[1] who has studied leadership for thirty years says "there are almost as many definitions as leadership as there are persons who have attempted to define the concept", but it is too complex and too variable to a phenomenon to be captured in any definition and every professional, management expert, researcher, theorist, economist, scientist, political orator, business executive, social worker and educationalist has defined leadership in his own way. Every one has ideas and opinions about leadership even children[2]. All agree that leadership is important but no one can define it to the satisfaction of the every one. Yukl (1981)[3] opined the numerous definitions of leadership that have been proposed appear to have little else in common. Though, in fact the terms has never been clearly defined, some of the Quotable definitions of leadership given by notable management scientists are enlisted hereunder:

> In the words of Koontz O'Donnell[4] "Leadership is the art or process of influencing people so that they will strive willingly and enthusiastically toward the achievement of group goals".

According to Reober Tannenbaum[5] leadership is the "interpersonal influence exercised in situation and directed, through the communication process towards the attainment of goals". Leadership is defined by Paul Hersay and K.H. Blachard[6] as "the process of influencing group activities towards the accomplishment of goals in a given situation."

Keith Davis[7] defines leadership as "Something a person does, not something he has"

According to G.R. Terry[8] "Leadership is the relationship in which one person, or the leader influences other to work together willingly on related tasks to attain that which the leader desires".

Peter Drucker is of the Opinion that "Leadership is the characteristic of an individual.

Alford Beatty says that "Leadership is the ability to secure desirable actions form a group of followers". Fiedler is of the viewed that "Leadership is the task of directing and coordinating task relevant to group activities"

> According to Chester Barnard "Leadership refers to the quality of the behaviour of the individuals where by they guide people in their activities in organized efforts". Hemphill, J.K. says that "Leadership is the initiation of acts which results in a consistent pattern of group interaction directed towards the solution of mutual problem". Keith Davis has further defined "Leadership as the ability to pursue others to seek defined objectives

enthusiastically. It is the human factor which binds a group together and motivates it towards goals.

Kochan, et al.[9] gave a similar definition but exemplifying the process of leadership as "influence process whereby O's actions change P's behaviour and P views the influence attempt as being legitimate and the change as being consistent with P's goals".

Agreeing with the definitions noted above Arnold[10] briefs leadership in simple terms saying that "Leadership is managing individual and group behaviour in organization."

Characteristics of Leadership

David C McCland[11] emphasis a strong drive for achievement as an important attribute for motivation and the quality which characterizes outstanding leaders. A leader shows the way by his own example. He is not a pusher, he pulls rather than pushes. Because of this, Keith Davis[12] enlists the following as the characteristics of leadership;

(i) Intelligence: Leaders tend to have somewhat higher intelligence than their followers.

(ii) Social maturity breadth: Leaders have a tendency to be emotionally mature and to have a broad range of interests.

(iii) Inner motivation and achievement drives: Leaders want to accomplish things; when they achieve one goal, they seek out another. They are not primarily dependent on outside forces for their motivation.

(iv) Human relations attitudes: Leaders are able to work effectively with other persons. They respect individuals and realize that to accomplish tasks they must be considerate of others.

Further, The characteristics of the leadership may also be studies as follows:

(i) Basically leadership is a quality present in individual. It may be inborn or developed by the individual, (ii) The individual who posses this quality has to show it through his behaviour, character and way of commanding, (iii) Leadership as a function of management is used to motivate the people by way of guiding them, (iv) Quality and function of leadership is performed by establishing relationship between the persons and the leader. Unless such a relationship exists the leader may not be successful in influencing people to act in a certain direction, (v) Influence the people (vi) The main function of leadership is to guide the subordinates in problem areas and in performance of their duties, (vii) Leaders direct the people towards organizational goals for their achievement, (viii) Above all leadership is one of the important functions of management required for accomplishment of organizational goals smoothly, (ix) Leader and Leadership can not exist without followers, (x) The way of leading the people depends mainly upon the situation. In some situations the leader has to pacify the followers while in some situations the leader is supposed to represent them.

Thus, the term 'leadership' when used in connection with management, does not refer to excelling, but to guiding others or their activities towards predetermined objectives or goals. The leader's acts are goal oriented. He uses his influence to achieve some desired goals. The primary task of a leader is to build a team for achievement of organizational objectives. This can be done by convincing people to follow him by participating in the organizational activities.

The list of desirable characteristics is a long one if the suggestions of all the important authorities are taken into account, but among them are the following:

(i) ***Self-confidence:*** The belief in one's own power to succeed in solving problems and one's own ability to deal effectively with difficult situations.

(ii) ***Drive:*** The urge and enthusiasm to stimulate action both personal and in other people.

(iii) ***Initiative:*** The ability to lead action without waiting to be promoted and to bring fresh thought to old problems.

(iv) ***Decisiveness:*** The ability to think positively and without vacillation and to act in the same way.

(v) ***Willingness to accept responsibility:*** This includes the acceptance of accountability for one's decisions and the consequent acts of oneself and one's staff.

(vi) ***Integrity:*** This includes trustworthiness and loyalty to one's organization and one's staff.

(vii) ***Judgment:*** The ability to analyse situation and formulate appropriate action. This includes choosing between different possible courses of action where choices present themselves.

(viii) ***Stamina:*** The ability to work long and hard without undue strain or stress.

(ix) ***Emotional Maturity:*** Includes self-discipline and self-control and the ability to analyse a situation without prejudice.

(x) ***Human Understanding:*** The ability to work with other people with understanding and sympathy; the willingness to listen to staff problems.[13]

Components of Leadership

Koontz O'Donnel[14] observes the following four as components of leadership.

1. **Power** : The first component of leadership pertains to power.

2. **Fundamental Understanding**: The second component of leadership concerns a fundamental understanding of people.

3. **Ability to Inspire** : The third component of leadership seems to be the rare ability to inspire followers to apply their full capabilities to a Project.

4. **Style of Leadership** : The fourth component of leadership has to do with the style of the leader and the climate he or she develop as a result.

Requirements of Leadership

According to Peter Drucker there are three requirements for leadership.

1. What distinguish the leader from misleader are his goals.
2. Second requirements is that leader sees his leadership as a responsibly, rather than rank and privilege. When things go wrong the real leader does not blame others.
3. Third requirements of leadership is to earn trust.

Dimensions of Leadership

Definitions given by various experts regarding Leadership have four dimensions:

1. **The accomplishment of goals** : The effective leader may have to deal with individual group and organization goal. Leader effectiveness typically is considered in terms of the degree of accomplishment of one or combination of these goals.

2. **Influencing followers** : This element of definition involves the importance of communication and understanding

the behaviour and performance of follower. The clarity and accuracy of communication affects the process behaviour and performance of follower.

3. **Situation:** The effectiveness of the leader and the selection of an effective leadership style depend on situation. It is likely to find one best way of leadership style that is panacea in all circumstances.

4. **Guiding and Directing** : The process of guiding and directing the behaviour of people in work equipment.

Importance of Leadership

Leadership is a matter of pushing people until they do what the leader wishes them to do. Leadership is primarily a matter of removing barriers so that people can act with freedom and independence. Leadership encourages and stimulates action from workers by innovating them in planning and decision making activities. Following points indicate the importance of leadership.

1. **Leadership influences to work more:** Main function of leadership is to influence others. This he does through showing his own interest in the work. He being positive towards the work can automatically make others work with the same interest and zeal.

2. **Leadership provides guidance and direction:** Main characteristic of leadership is the ability to guide and direct the followers. The leader guides the followers away from the problem areas and leads as well as directs them on right path to do the jobs effectively.

3. **Leadership leads the followers :** Some people are not in a position to work independently. The require some one to lead and guide them. They believe that they can do better if they are led by some one. This someone is a leader. The leader, therefore, works himself and automatically others follow him.

4. Leadership discovers new methods: The has to try to implement organization's policies and programmes designed to achieve objectives. He has to resort to various methods for getting the jobs done by his team. Many times, existing methods may not be capable of providing motivation. In such circumstances the leader has to discover new methods and initiate them for the purpose.

5. Development of team Spirit : A leader is a person who leads a group. The group members believe in him. The leader, by this, induces, persuades his members to work honestly to give maximum contribution. The leader has to develop team spirit in the group because, without this, work cannot be done effectively. Once the leader is successful in developing team spirit in the group, half of the work is as good as done.

6. Creation of Confidence: The leader, in order to get the work done properly, has to take his followers in confidence. He has to listen to their problems and difficulties and has to solve them, by giving proper guidance and direction. This creates confidence in the follower workers. He has further, to give them proper training, education and clear instructions. Thus an employee is made more confident to perform for better them others.

7. Excellent time management: A leader is further responsible to make maximum and proper use of the available time, as he has to complete the assigned jobs in stipulated time period, he therefore, cannot afford wastage of time on any other job or on any unproductive activity. He therefore, has to see that his work force does not get bored and exhausted. All this can be done if the time management is made properly and efficiently. Naturally leadership leads to excellent time management.

8. Builds high moral among people: High moral among the employees is essential for making organization successful. It is the duty or responsibility of a leader to develop and maintain high morale among the employees. Moral denotes the attitude of employees towards organization, its objectives, management and their willingness to offer their honest contribution to the organization. The employees having high moral are found to be happy and satisfied in an organization. Rather high morale is the outcome of worker's happiness and satisfaction.

9. Effective Utilization of Resources: A leader utilizes human and non human resources to maximum extent for productive purposes. At the same time he uses both resources efficiently and effectively. It leads to maximum wastage, some times there would be elimination of wastages also.

Leadership Skills

To satisfy the characteristics discussed earlier, Katz talks of three types of skills that are recognized by all managers.

1. Technical Skill : Refers to a person's knowledge and ability in any type of process or technique. Examples are the skills learned by accountants, engineers, typists, tool makers etc. This skill is a distinguishing features of job performance at the operating level; but as employees are promoted to leadership responsibilities, their technical skill becomes proportionately less important as showed in figure. They increasingly depend on the technical skills of their subordinates and in many cases have never practiced some of the technical skills that they supervise.

2. Human skill: Human skill is the ability to work effectively as group member and to build cooperative efforts within the team he leads.

3. Conceptional skill: It is the ability to see the organization as a whole. It includes recognizing how the various functions of the organization depend on one another. It makes the individual to be aware how changes in any one part of the organization affect all the others. Thus, it extends to visualizing the relationship of the individual business to the industry, the community and the political, social and economic forces of the nation as a whole.

FIGURE

Variations in Use of Leadership Skills at Different Organizational Levels

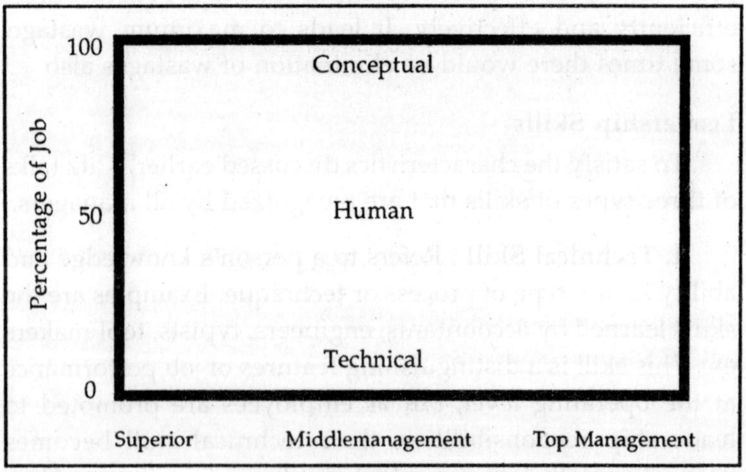

Leadership Qualities

What qualities a leader should possess is a subject of different opinions among distinguished thinkers which is evident from the discussion that follows:

F.M. Viscount[15] has chosen six basic qualities of a leader as follows:

(1) Courage, (2) Will Power (3) judgement, (4) Flexibility, (5) Knowledge and (6) Integrity

Odway Tead[16] on the other hand has listed the following ten qualities of a good leader:

1. Physical and Nervious Energy, 2. Enthusiasm, 3. Sence of Purpose and Direction, 4. Technical Mastery, 5. Integrity, 6. Technical Skill, 7. Friendliness and Affection, 8. Decisivenses, 9. Intelligency and 10. Faith

Henry Fayol[17] treats the following as qualities of a good leader: 1. Healthy and Physical Fitness, 2. Intelligence and Mutual Vigour 3. Moral Qualities 4. Knowledge and 5. Managerial ability.

Cheter I. Barnard[18] has observed the below as the qualities of a good leader.

1. Vitality and Endurance, 2. Decisiveness, 3. Persuasiveness, 4. Stability, 5. Intellectual Capacity and 6. Knowledge.

George R. Terry[19] gives the following qualities:

1. Energy, both mental and physical required for a job.
2. Emotional stability which enables a leader to act with self confidence, avoid anger and deal with his subordinates with understanding.
3. Knowledge of human relations which requires an understanding of human behaviour.
4. Empathy which enables him to look at things objectively and form another's view-point.
5. Objectively which prevents him from getting emotionally involved.

6. Personal motivation that is enthusiasm within himself to get the job done.
7. Communication skill that is the ability to talk and write clearly and force-fully.
8. Teaching ability which will help him to develop and inspire his subordinates.
9. Social Skill which will help him to understand and know their strength and weakness and presents him as a friendly and approachable person and
10. Technical competence which provides him with an effective working knowledge and insight of the operations and his guidance.

Thus, to be an effective leader, he must posses sound knowledge of human behaviour, attitudes and both individual and organizational goals. Majority of all these must necessarily be possessed by a successful leader. That leader must also be a capable handler of interpersonal relations. Robert Dublin says :[20]

"All people are potential leaders. And, given the desire and opportunity, people can develop into effective ones .... A group abhors confusion, including the confusion resulting from being leaderless. Every organization has many people in it who can exercise leadership, at least temporarily, than there are positions of leadership to be filled. It is often in situations of the crisis, where an individual, not previously known to possess such qualities, becomes a leader, that officials of an organization learn where the potential leadership skills are to be found."

As group goals and tasks change, new leaders and shifts in power occur. Leadership in a group depends on the group standards and what leadership rules are acceptable. Although no set of absolute traits may be identified, the individuals who possess abilities to led others must have certain attributes to help them in performing their leadership roles.

The following authors give different qualities of a leader and his or her behaviours. In the opinion of Viscount Slim, the main leadership traits are : Courage, Will power, Judgment, Flexibility, Knowledge and Integrity.

Ordway Tead is of the view that the qualities of a leader are : physical and nervous energy, Enthusiasm, Sense of purpose and direction, Technical Mastery, Friendliness and affection, Decisiveness, Integrity, Intelligence and Faith.

Chester Barnard thinks that a leader should have : Vitality and endurance, Decisiveness, Persuasiveness, Stability in behaviour, Intellectual ability and Knowledge.

According to Hill, the characteristics of a good leader are: Self-confidence, Moral qualities, Self-sacrifice, Paternalism, Fairness, Initiative, Decisiveness, Dignity and Knowledge of men.

Nitish R. De has given the following characteristics of a leader; A great deal of physical and nervous energy, endurance and vigor of body and mind, Readiness to shoulder responsibility and ability to discharge it, Unfaltering friendliness and affection, Tolerance and patience, Sense of fairplay and justice, A high degree of integrity, Knowledge of men, Dicisiveness and initiative and Ability to face through weather, opposition, callousness and ridicule.

According to George Terry, the qualities of a leader should have; Energy, Emotional stability, Knowledge of human relations, Personal motivation, Communication skill, Teaching ability, Social skill and Technical competence.

Most writers are of the view that a "successful" leader has an above-average education is active in social organization, and has high moral standards. Such characteristics as the ability to adjust, good appearance, and need for achievement, assertiveness and fear of failure have also been reported as essential leadership traits.

THE NATURE OF LEADERSHIP

Leadership is part of management, but not all of it. Managers are required to plan and organized, for example, but all we ask of leaders is that they influence others to follow. The fact that they influence other to follow is no guarantee that they are going in the right direction. This means that strong leaders can be weak managers because they weak in planning or some other managerial duty. Though they can get their group going, they just cannot get them going directions that serve organizational objectives.

The reverse is also possible. A manager can be a weak leader and still be an acceptable manager, especially if one happens to be managing people who have strong drivers to work. This combination of circumstances is less likely, and usually we expect an excellent manager also to have reasonably high leadership ability.

Even though leadership is something a person does, it should not be confused with mere activity. Aggressiveness and constant interaction with others will not guarantee good leadership. At times the appropriate leadership action is to stay in the background keeping pressure off the group, to keep quite so that others may talk, to be calm in times of uproar, to hesitate, and to delay decisions.

Leaders are a key human resources in any organization. We usually of companies competing by means of their products, but they probably compete more by means of their leaders than their products. Better leaders develop better employees, and the two together develop better products;

therefore, and employer who develops better leaders contributes more to society and gains a competitive advantage. Just as a company requires capital and modern physical facilities, it also requires a continuous supply of competent leaders to fill vacancies caused by death, retirement, and registration. A growing company requires an even larger supply of leaders.

It is evident that leadership is situational. In one situation, action A may be the best cluster of leadership acts, but in the next situation, action B will be the best cluster. To try to have all an organization's leaders fit a standard pattern will suppress creative difference and be inefficient as well, because many square pegs will be trying to fit into round holes. Leadership is part of a complex system, so there is no simple answer to the riddle "what makes a leader?"

Leaders as followers. The fact is sometimes overlooked that, with few exceptions, leaders in organizations are also followers. They nearly always report to someone else. Even the president reports to a board of directors. Leaders must be able to wear both hats gracefully, to be able to relate both upward and downward. They need validation from higher authority just as much as they need support from followers. In formal organizations of several levels, the ability to follow is one of the first requirements for good leadership. It is the key that unlocks the door to leadership opportunities and keeps the leader in balance with the rest of the organization.

NATURE AND FUNCTIONS OF LEADER

Leader is not a lay-figure. He has much to do. The functions may be relatively straight-forward. In the wake of vast and rapid technological changes leader has to perform multifarious functions. Some of the important functions the leader performs are given under :

1. Leader develops team work[21]: The three vital determinates of team work are the leader, subordinates and the environment. These factors are interdependent. It is the leader's responsibility to make the environment conductive to work. He inculcates the sense of collectivism in employees to work as a team.
2. Leader is a representative of subordinates : He is an intermediary between the work groups and top management. They are called linking pins by Rensis Likert[22].
3. Leader is an appropriate Counselor: Quite often people in the work place need counseling to eliminate the emotional disequilibrium that is created sometimes in them. He removes barriers and stumbling blocks to effective performance.
4. Uses Power Properly : If a leader is to effectively achieve the goals expected of him, he must have power and authority to act in a way that will stimulate a positive response from the workers.

A leader depending on the situation exercises different types of power viz., reward power, conceive power, legitimate power, represent power, and expert power. Besides the formal basis the informal basis of power also has a more powerful impact on organizational effectiveness.[23] No leader is effective unless the subordinates obey his orders.

5. Leader manages the time well : Time is precious and vital but often overlooked in management. There are three dimensions of time, boss-imposed time, system-imposed-time and self-imposed-time, that are prominent in literature. Because the leader has through knowledge of the principles of time management such as time preparing charts,

scheduling techniques etc., he is in a position to utilize the time productivity in the organizations.[24]

6. Strive for effectiveness : Quite frequently the managers are workaholic and too busy with petty things to address to major details of effectiveness. To fill the gap, some times leader throws his concerted effort to bring effectiveness by encouraging and nurturing team work, by better time management and by the proper use of power.[25]

Leadership is rather examined in personal characteristics than in terms of activities. Herbert G. Hicks[26] refers the following as common leadership activities.

1. *Arbitrating:* Often members disagree on the best decision for an organizational matter. An effective leader often will resolve such disagreement by arbitrating on making the decision on the course of action to be taken.

2. *Suggesting:* Suggestions are often employed by an adroit leader for a long-term. Suggestions is likely to be a powerful tool in the manager's kit.

3. *Supplying objectives:* A manager often personally supplies the objectives for the organization. The manager must see that the organization is always supplied with suitable objectives.

4. *Catalyzing:* In organizations some force is required to start or accelerate movement. A leader is expected to provide such a force.

5. *Providing Security:* In organizations personal security is often a significant factor. A leader can provide a large measure of security by maintaining a positive and optimistic attitude even the face of adversities.

6. *Representing:* A leader usually treated as the representative of the organization.

7. *Inspiring:* Many persons work more productively in organizations when their leader keeps them known that the work they do is worthwhile and of important.

8. *Praising:* Managers can help to satisfy the needs by their sincere praise.

The functions discussed above are of an ideal leader. Though an ordinary leader cannot perform all these functions, but he should do his best in the interest of subordinates. Hence, Stogdill[27] is right in saying that "Leadership is consistent with problems of human performance and interaction".

Thus, it can be said that a leader has the function of leading the group of his subordinates. As leader, he has not only to show the way but also to lead the group towards it. Because of this, Haiman[28] says, "It is leadership for the mutual objectives and that is not sheer weight of authority or power".

REFERENCES

1. Stogdill, R.M. *Hand Book of Leadership*, Force Press, New York, 1974, p. 7.
2. Cartwright, D. and Zander, A.F., *Group Dynamics Research*, Harper & Row, New York, 1953.
3. Yuk 1, G.A., *Leadership in Organizations*, Englewood Cliffs, N.J., Prentice-Hall, New Delhi, 1981, p. 1.
4. Koontz, O'Donnell, et al., *Management*, 8th edition, Mc Graw-Hill International Book Company, New York, 1984, p. 506.
5. Tannenbaum, Reober, Irwing R. Wescheir and Fred Massarik, *Leadership and Organisation, A Behavioural Science Approach*, McGraw-Hill Book Company, Inc., New York, 1961, p. 24.
6. Paul Hersay and Blanchard, K.H., *op. cit*, 1977.
7. Keith, Davis., *op. cit.*, 1975, p. 100.
8. George R. Terry and Richard D. Irwin, *Principles of Management*, Inc., Homewood, Illinois, 1968, p. 45.

9. Kochan, Schmidt, & Decotiis, *op. cit.*, 1975, p. 285.
10. Daniel C., et al., *op. cit.*, 1983, pp. 287-303.
11. David C. McCelland, *The Achieving Society*, D. Van Nostrand Company Inc., 1961.
12. Davis Keith, *op. cit.*, 1972, pp. 102-104.
13. Eyre, E.G. *Mastering Basic Management*, I edition, Macmillan Master Services, Hong Kong, 1982, p.148.
14. Koontz, O'Donnel, et. al. *op. cit.*, 1984, pp. 506-507.
15. Viscount, P.M., Leadership, *The Journal of the British Institute of Management*, Management Publications Ltd., Volume 30, No. 1, Jan, 1962, pp. 37-41.
16. Tead Ordway, *The Art of Leadership*, McGraw- Hill Book Company, New York, 1935, p. 93.
17. Fayal, Henry, *General And Industrial Management*, I Edition, Sir Issac Pitman & Sons Ltd., 1949, pp. 76-77.
18. Barnard, I. Chester., *The Functions of the Executive*, Harvard University Press, Cambridge. London, 1968.
19. Geroge R. Terry., *op. cit.*, 1968, pp. 461-463.
20. Dubin Robert, *Organization Behaviour*, Prentice Hall, 1997, pp 66.
21. Davis, Keith., *op. cit*, p. 447.
22. Rensis Likert, *New Patterns of Management*, McGraw Hill Book Company, New York. 1961. pp. 113-115.
23. Gerald G. Banchman, David G. Bowers and Phillip M. Marcers, "Bases of Supervisory Power: A Comparative Study in Five Setting in Arnold, S. Tannebaum (ed). *Control in Organizations*, McGraw Hill Book Company, New York, 1968, p. 336.
24. Richard M. Hodgets., *Modern Human Relations*, The Dryden Press Hindale. Illinois, 1980, p. 271.
25. *Ibid.*, pp. 259-277.
26. Hicks G. Herbert and Ray Gullett, C., *The Management of Organization*, 3rd Edition, Book Company, New York, pp. 447-449.
27. Stodgill, R.M., & Coons, A.E., *op. cit*, 1957.
28. Haimann, theo., *Professional Management Theory and Practice*, 3rd edition, Eurasia Publishing House Pvt. Ltd., New Delhi, 1962, p. 144.

3

THEORIES OF LEADERSHIP

Leadership is complex and multidimensional in character and as such none can dare to jump prematurely to prescriptions and generalization from the leadership research. In fact, most of the leadership studies are concerned with this single issue—what is the theory of leadership? Literature on leadership is voluminous are much but it is confusing as well as contradictory.[1] In an effort to clarify the leadership concept it is appropriate to consider it in the light of several approaches used to investigate leadership and to explain its nature.

There are several distinct theoretical bases for leadership. In the beginning, leaders were felt to be born, not made. This evolved into what is known as the trait theory of leadership.[2] The exponents of trait theory were Thomas Carlyle, Frederick Nietzche and William James. Their studies were based on an attempt to identify the traits that leaders possess. According to them leaders are born but not made. This approach is traditional one and often it has also been called as the "Great Man" theory of leadership.

Ralph Stogdill,[3] one of the premiere leadership researchers, surveyed more than 5000 leadership studies and concluded that there are no consistent patterns of traits that characterize leaders in all situations. However, he did reach some general conclusions in the following five areas which valuable for study and thought.

1. Intelligence and Scholarship.
2. Physical traits
3. Personality
4. Social Status and experience, and
5. Task orientation.

Edwine Ghiselli[4] has conducted extensive research on the relationship between personality and motivational traits and leadership effectiveness. He studied over 300 managers from 90 different companies and his findings suggest that the following personality traits range from being very important to unimportant in relation to leadership success.

TABLE 1

Personal Traits of Leaders

Abilities	*Personal Traits*	*Motivations*
• Supervising ability	• Self assurance	• Need for Occupational achievement
• Intelligence	• Decisiveness	• Self actualization
• Initiative	• Masculinity/ Femininity	• Power over others
	• Maturity	• High financial Reward
	• Work Class affinity	• Job security

Source: Ghiselli, Edwine E., *op cit.*, pp. 120-130.

Keith Davis[5] has pulled together the following four traits that are shared by most successful leaders:

1. Intelligence,
2. Social maturity and breadth,
3. Inner motivation and achievement drive, and,
4. Human relation attitudes.

Research efforts at isolating these traits resulted in a number of dead ends. For instance review of twenty different studies identified nearly eighty leadership traits, but only five of these traits were common to four or more of the investigations. If the search was intended to identify a set of traits that would always differentiate leaders from followers and effective from ineffective leaders, the search obviously failed. Perhaps it was a bit optimistic to believe that there could be consistent and unique traits that would apply across the board to all effective leaders no matter whether they were in charge of the Hell's Angles, the Mormon Tabernacle Choir, General Electric, the CIA, the Ku Klux Klan, or the Congress of Racial Equality.

If, however, the research was intended to identify traits that were consistently associated with leadership, the results can be interpreted in a more impressive light. For example, intelligence, dominance, self-confidence, high energy level, and task relevant knowledge are five traits that show consistently positive correlations with leadership. But "positive correlations" should not be interpreted to mean "definitive predictors." The correlations between these traits and leadership have generally been in the range of + 0.25 to +0.3.5. -interesting results but not earth shattering.[6]

The results represent the conclusions based on seventy years of trait research. These modest correlations coupled with the inherent limitations of the trait approach-it overlooks the needs of followers, generally fails to clarify the relative importance of various traits, doesn't separate cause from effect (for example, are leaders self-confident or does success as a leader build self-confidence?), and ignores situational factors-naturally led researchers in other directions. Although there has been some resurgent interest in traits during the past decade, 7 major movement away from traits began as early as the 1940s. Leadership research from the late 1940s through the mid 1960s emphasized the preferred behavioural styles that leaders demonstrated.

The earliest approaches to the study of leadership focused not on the process of influencing others, but on the personal characteristics of the leaders themselves. Philosophers and researchers alike tried to determine what traits-physical, intellectual and personal-distinguish leaders from followers (some times called "The Great Man" approach.) Early studies revealed a perplexingly large number of traits related to leadership success. However, because researchers found no single small set of traits that consistently predicts leadership success in a variety of situations, the trait approach lost credibility in 1950's and 1960's /Experts now recognize that certain traits increase the likelihood that person will be an effective leader, but they do not guarantee effectiveness and relative importance of different traits depends on the nature of the leadership situation.

Some research suggests that personality traits such as age, height, intelligence, academic achievement, judgment ability, and insight are associated with effective leadership (Tosiet al, 2000). Still other researchers identify creativity, emotional balance, nonconformity and diplomacy (Inancevich and Matteson, 1990:388). However, no specific traits seems to be correlated with leadership in all situations. There are several explanations for such results.

First, just because a person has a particular single trait is not a sufficient condition to be in a leadership position or a management job and be successful in it. The person must want the job, seek it, and want to be effective. In addition, traits do not operate alone, but in consonance with other factors.

Second reason that made these research studies produce very divergent results is that the studies have been done in too many different situations. Traits may be related to effectiveness in certain situations but not in others.

Third there is also a possibility that the trait research tended to focus on very specific traits instead of more general factors. After a careful review of several traits studies, it appears that if specific traits groups were grouped into general classes of factors.

Trait theories of leadership attempt to identify the traits and/or inherent attributes of leaders, regardless of the leaders situation or circumstances, as well as the impact of the straits and /or styles on the followers. Trait theories focused on a physical attributes, personality, and abilities. Recently, a renewed intensive in type I theories has focused attention on the distinctions between leaders and managers, as well as on charismatic leadership. The implications of Type I theories for organizations involve selection issues rather than training and development issues.

The first studies of leadership attempted to identify what physical attributes personality characteristics, and abilities distinguished leaders .from other members of a group. The physical attributes considered have been height, weight, physique, energy, health, appearance and even age. This line of research yielded some interesting findings. However, very few valid generalizations emerged from this line of inquiry. Therefore, there is insufficient evidence to conclude that leaders can be distinguished from followers on the basis of physical attributes.[7]

Leader personality characteristics that have been examined include originality, adaptability, introversion-extroversion, dominance, self-confidence, integrity, conviction, mood optimism, and emotional control. There is some evidence that leaders may be more adaptable and self-confident that the average group member.

With regard to leader abilities, attention has been devoted to such constructs as social skills, intelligence, scholarship, speech fluency, cooperativeness, and insight. In this area, there is some evidence that leaders are more intelligent, verbal, and cooperative and have a higher level of scholarship than the average group member.

These conclusions suggest traits leaders possess, but the findings are neither strong nor uniform. For each attribute or trait claimed to distinguish leaders from followers, there were always at least one or two studies with contradictory findings. This suggests a limitation in being able to identify universal, distinguishing attributes of leaders.

If we were to describe a leader based on the general connotations presented in today's media, we might list qualities such as intelligence, charsma, decisiveness, enthusiasm, strength, bravery, integrity, self confidence, and so on-possibly elicting the conclusion that effective leaders must be one part Boy Scout and two parts Jesus Christ. The search for characteristics such as those listed that would differentiate leaders from non-leaders occupied the early psychologists who studies leadership.

Is it possible to isolate one or more personality, social, physical, or intellectual characteristics in individuals we generally acknowledge as leadership - Mahatma Gandhi, Martin Luther King, Jr. Joan of Arc. Adolph Hitler, Winston Churchill, General Douglas, MacArthur, John F. Kennedy, Lee Iacocca, Ted Turner, Donald Trump—that nonreaders to not possess? We may agree that these individuals meet our definition of a leader, but they represent individuals with utterly different characteristics. If the concept of traits were to be proved valid, there must be following specific characteristics that all leaders should possess.[8]

Characteristics of Trait Theory

1. Capacity- refers to an individual's ability to solve problems, make judgment, and generally work harder. Specific traits are intelligence, alertness, verbal facility, originality, and judgment.

2. Achievement- effective leaders tend to do better in academic work, have more knowledge, and accomplish more in athletics that in-effective leaders.

3. Responsibility- is another general characteristic of effective leaders. Specific traits that reflect responsibility are dependability, initiative, persistence, aggressiveness, self-confidence and a desire to excel.

4. Participation and involvement- are higher for effective leaders than for ineffective ones, Effective leaders tend be more active and more sociable, have greater capacity to adapt to different situations, and show higher levels of cooperation than less effective leaders.

5. Status- is the relative position or standing of a person in a group that causes respect or deference toward them. Effective leaders have higher socio-economic status and are more popular than ineffective leaders.

Thus, the trait approach, while interesting and intuitively appealing, does not seem to be very efficient for identifying and predicting leadership potential (Ivancevich and Mateson, 1990, 390).

Behavioural Theories

The inability to strike "gold" in the trait mines led researches to look at the behaviours that specific leaders exhibited. They wondered if there were something unique in the way that effective leaders behave. For example, do they trend to be more democratic than autocratic?

Because of the widespread in consistencies of trait studies of leadership effectiveness[9] and stimulated by researchers switched their emphasis from the individual leader to the group which is being led. In the group approach, leadership is viewed more in terms of th[9] Terry, G.r. & Franklin, S.G., Principles of Management, 8th edition, All India Traveler Book Seller, New Delhi, 1984, p. 331

During 1950's the dis-satisfaction with the traits approach to leadership led behavioural scientist to focus their attention on the actual leader behaviour viz., what leader does and how he/she does it. It analyses the various functions which people carry out when they are in leadership position.

There are three well known behavioural approaches of leadership. The studies at Iowa University attempted by lewin Lipitt and white (1939),[10] studies at Ohio State University conducted by Stogdill and Coons (1951)[11] and the Michigan studies by Katz, Maccoby and Morse (1950).[12] In all these studies the authors distinguished successful leader from unsuccessful leader by their particular style of leadership. This approach increases confidence in the existence of some underlying patterns in leader behaviour and provides us with useful method for describing and analyzing what leaders actually do.

By the late 1940's most of the leadership research had changed from trait theory to focus on what the leader did. In the continuing quest to find the one best leadership style in all situations, researchers attempted to identify the differences in the behaviour of the effective leaders versus the in effective leaders. Behavioural leadership Theories attempt to determine distinctive style used by effective leaders.

Two major dimensions of leader behaviour emerged from this body of research one deals with how leaders get the job done and the other deals with how leaders treat and interact with their subordinates. Three of there models that developed from this research are the Ohjo state model, the University of Michigan Model and the leadership grid model.

Following World War II, Ohio State University researchers conducted one of the most widely known leadership studies to explore the determinants of successful leadership behaviour and investigate the various leadership styles on group performance and job satisfaction.[13]

These investigators identified two major factors or dimensions with which managers-leaders are concerned: Initiating structure and consideration.[14]

Initiating structure refers to the extent to which a leader is likely to define and structure his or her role and those of subordinates in the search for goal attainment. It includes behaviour that attempts to organize work, work relationship and goals. Consideration is described as the extent to which a person is likely to have job relationships that are characterized by mutual trusts, respect for subordinates' ideas and regard to their feelings.[15]

Yulk (1971)[16] and stogdill[17] have found that subordinates report higher levels of satisfaction with a leader who is considerate than with initiating structure. Neither consideration nor initiating structure has been found to be consistently related to in an effort to describe what leaders actually do, researchers at Ohio state University analyzed the results of questionnaires they administered to a sample of leaders and followers. From this, they concluded that leadership behaviour consists of two broadly defined dimensions i.e. Consideration and initiating structure. Consideration behaviours involve being friendly and supportive by listening to employees' problems, supporting their actions, "going to bat" for them, and getting their input on variety of issues.

Initiating-Structure behaviours involve defining and structuring leader-subordinating roles through activities such as scheduling, defining work tasks, setting deadlines, criticizing poor work, getting employees to accept work standards, and resolving problems.

Early studies found the "Hi-Hi leaders" those ranking high in both dimensions, are most effective, although results were in consistent. Subsequent research found that there may not be a simple relationship between the two dimensions and effectiveness. The only rehable funding has been that leaders exhibiting consideration behaviours tend to have more satisfied subordinates. Relationships between two dimensions and effectiveness appear to depend on the situation.

Iowa Studies of Leadership: The initial attempts to classify and study the effect of different styles of leader behaviour were carried out at the University of Iowa (in late 1930's by Ronald, Lippit and Ralph K. White under the general directions of Kurt Lewin at the University of Iowa).[18] The Iowa theorists focused on decision-making component of the leader's behaviour and classified leaders into three different types-the authoritarian, democratic and lassize-faire-according to situations.

The authoritarian leader is very directive and allowed no participation. This leader tends to give individual attention when praising and criticizing but tries to be friendly or impersonal rather than openly hostile. The democratic leader encourages group discussion and decision-making. He tries to be objective in his praise or criticism and to be one of the group in spirit. The laissize-faire gives complete freedom to the group and he essentially provides no leadership.[19]

By and large, not only the Iowa studies are important in the sense that they have helped attention to leadership behaviour as a critical focus of study, but also they have developed a helpful basis for describing and classifying alternative leadership styles.[20]

Michigan Studies : Another group of scientists at the University of Michigan was also involved in research on leadership effectiveness. The approach adopted by the Michigan researchers (e.g. Katz, Maccoby & Morse, 1950) was first to identify leaders who are acknowledge to be either effective or ineffective and than to study the behaviour of these leaders in a search for patterns of behaviour that might differentiate the effective and ineffective leaders.[21]

At about the same time the Ohio State studies were being conducted, researchers at the University of Michigan were also studying leadership effectiveness from behavioural perspective. They two compared effective leaders to less-effective leaders and came up with two dimensions of leadership behaviour, which they labeled "task oriented behaviours" and "relationship oriented behaviours".

Task oriented behaviours : The researchers found that effective managers engage in task-oriented behaviours such as planning, scheduling work, coordinating employee activities, and providing necessary supplies, equipment, and technical assistance-al designed primarily and specifically to get tasks completed and goals met. This task-oriented behaviour appears to correspond to the initiating structure dimension identified in the Ohio state studies.

Relationship-oriented behaviour : The researchers also found that effective managers employ relationship oriented behaviours, such as being considerate, supportive, and helpful to subordinates by showing trust and confidence, listening to employees' problems and suggestion, showing appreciation for contributions, and supporting employees' careers. There relationship-oriented behaviours correspond to the consideration behaviours of the Ohio state research.

The conclusions drawn in this regard by various researchers are more or less similar to consideration and initiating structure. But generally the employee-oriented leadership generates higher levels of employee satisfaction. However, there is no consistent evidence that either leadership style results in higher levels of productivity.

Rinsis Likert, a management theorist and leader of the Michigan Institute for social Research, summarized the research by concluding that the most effective managers engage in both dimensions of leadership behaviour by getting employees involved in the operation of their departments or divisions in a positive and constructive manner, setting general goals, providing fairly loose supervision and recognizing their contributions. He called these managers employee-centred leaders. Less effective leaders are mostly directive in their approaches and most concerned with closely directing employees, explaining work procedures, and monitoring progress in task accomplishment; these he call Job-centred Leaders.

Managerial grid theory: Another personal-behaviour approach is the Managerial Grid. Robert Blake and Jane Mouton proposed that leadership style could be plotted on a two-dimensional grid: on the horizontal axis is **"concern for production"** and on the vertical axis is **"concern for people"** This grid is presented in Figure 1.

Individual are asked questions about their leadership style and based on the responses, are placed at the appropriate point on the grid. Blake and Mouton,use the Managerial Grid as a framework to help managers learn what their leadership style is an to track their movement toward the ideal (9, 9) team management style.

Five specific leadership styles are used to highlight different approaches to leading others. Of course, these are only five of the many possible styles of leadership that can be and are utilized.

Impoverished: Exertion of minimum effort to get required work done is appropriate to sustain organization membership. Here, a minimum effort to accomplish the work is exerted by the leader.

Task: Efficiency in operations results from arranging conditions of work in such a way that human elements interfere to a minimum degree. Here, the leader concentrates on task efficiency but shows little regard for the development and morale of subordinates.

Country Club: Thoughtful attention to need of people for satisfying relationship leads to a comfortable, friendly organization atmosphere and work tempo. Here, the leader focuses on being supportive and considerate of employees. However, task efficiency is not a primary concern of this easygoing style.

Middle-of-the road: Adequate organization performance is possible through balancing the necessity to get out work with maintaining morale of people at a satisfactory level. In short adequate task efficiency and satisfactory morale are the goals of this style.

Team: Work accomplished is from committed people; interdependence through a 'common stake' in organization purpose leads to relationships of trust and respect. Here, the leader facilitates production and morale by coordinating and integrating work-related activities.

Blake and Mouton assume that the leader who is a 9,9 individual would be using the most effective style; however, defining a 9,9 leader for every type of job is very difficult. Blake and Mouton imply that a managerial development program can move leaders toward a 9,9 style. They recommend six management development phases (laboratory seminar groups, team building, inter-group processes, goal setting, goal feedback, evaluation) to aid the manager in acquiring concern for fellow employees and the expertise to accomplish objectives such as productivity and quality.

The longevity of the managerial grid method suggests that it is more than a fad to practicing managers. Thus, it would appear that more rigorous studies of what it can and cannot accomplish are required. Only by properly studying this approach can those interested in implementing it as a development method generally understand how it can change employee behaviour.

The Managerial Grid

The Ohio State leadership studies and the subsequent Japanese leadership approaches were behavioural formulations. Robert Blake developed an attitudinal formulation called the Managerial Grid. The two underlying dimensions of the grid are labeled. Concern for Production and Concern for People. These two attitudinal dimensions are coupled through an interaction process. The five distinct managerial styles shown in Figure paralleled five orientations to interpersonal relationships of fight (9.1), flight (1,1) depending (1,9), paring (5,5) and work (9,9) observed in previous clinical practice by Bion.

The organization man manager (5.5) works for adequate organizational performance by balancing getting work done and maintaining morale. This manager goes along to get along, conforming to and maintaining the status quo. The authority-obedience manager (9,1), emphasizes production and works to achieve high levels of efficiency in operations by minimizing any interference from the human element. Production maximization is the hallmark of this manager. The country club manager (1,9) gives thoughtful attention to the needs of people and their relationships so as to create a comfortable working environment. Good feelings are the hallmark of this manager. The team manager (9,9) emphasizes high levels of work accomplishment through committed, trustworthy people; there is no trade off between people and production. Finally, the improvershed manager (1,1) exerts the minimum effort to get essential work done while maintaining organizational membership. This style of management is similar to the liaises-faire style and is a form of abdication of responsibility.

The Managerial Grid is distinguished from the original Ohio State research in two important ways. First, it has attitudinal overtones that are not present in the original research. Whereas the LBDQ aims to describe behaviour, the grid address both behaviour and the attitude of the leader. Second, the Ohio State approach is fundamentally descriptive and no evaluative, whereas the grid is normative and prescriptive. Specifically, the grid evaluates the team manager (9,9) as the very best style of managerial behaviour. This is the basis on which the grid has been used for team building and leadership training in organizational development. As an organizational development method, the grid aims to transform the leadership structure of the organization and the manner in which teams throughout the organization are led unmanaged.[22]

Both the trait and behavioural approaches proved to fall short of a comprehensive and adequate theory of leadership style. Each of the theories attempted to isolated broad dimensions of leadership behaviour and indulge profusely

Concern for Production

1.9 Management thoughtful attention satisfying relationship leads to a comfortable friendly organization atmosphere tempo.		9.9 Management work accomplishment is from committed people interdependence through a common stake in organization purposes leads to relationships of trust and respect.
	5.5 Management adequate organization performance is possible through balancing the necessity to get out work while	
1.1 Management exertion of minimum effort to get required work done is appropriate to sustain organization membership.		9.1 Management efficiency in operations resulting from arranging conditions of work in such a way that human elements interfere to a minimum degree.

in over-simplification. The logic behind fallacious reasoning appears to be that multi-dimensions confound that interpretation of leadership bahaviour and complicate the research designs developed to test the particular theory.[23]

One of the best known discussion of contingency or alternatives are being explored. For instance, John Miner[24] was very critical of leadership theory and then proposed that it be dropped altogether.

The time seems ripe for new thinking and new theories, new research methods and new applications for leadership studies. A social learning approach seems to be one way to meet this challenge. In the regard situational leadership was developed by Tannenbaum and Schmidt some years ago[25]. They mentioned that three variables should be analysed; forces within the leader; forces in the followers; and forces in the situation. This approach to leadership emphasizes flexibility and sensitivity to the situation in which the leader and the group find themselves.

Contingency Theories

The basic idea behind contingency theories of leadership is that leadership effectiveness depends upon the existence of a 'fit' between the leader's behaviour and the demands of the situation. This basic notion is diagrammed in Figure 1.

FIGURE 1

Leaders Behaviour Fit

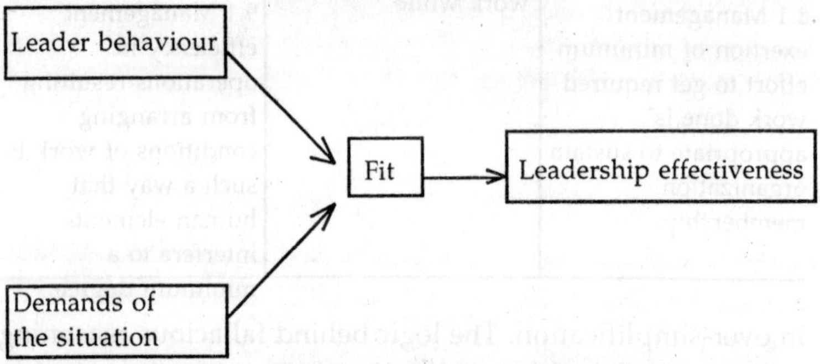

The situational theme of leadership is highly fascinating, but is certainly a challenging orientation to implement. An effective leader must be flexible enough to adopt to the differences among subordinates and situations. Leadership effectiveness depends upon the fit between personality, task, power, attitudes and perceptions. On the lines of this new and sophisticated conception, some elegant theories have been developed. They are:

1. Fielder's contingency model
2. House's Path-Goal Model,
3. Life Cycle theory of leadership,
4. Vroom's and Yetton Normative model.

Fielder's Contingency Model: To test the hypothesis that he has formulated from previous research finding, Fiedler developed what he called a Contingency model of leadership effectiveness. This model contains the relationship between leadership style and the favorableness of the situation. Situational favourableness was described by fielder in terms of three empirically derived dimensions:

(a) The leader-member relationship which is the most critical variable in determining the situation's favourableness.

(b) The Degree of task structure which is the second most important input into the favourableness of the situation; and

(c) The leader's position power obtained through formal authority which is the third most critical dimension of the situation.[26]

Neither trait nor the early behavioural approaches to leadership were able to identify conclusively a single best style of leadership. Infact, the most effective leadership style depends on the situation a leader faces. Several models that address contingency factors, include situational leadership theory. Fielder's contingency theory; path goal theory, and Vroon-Yetton-Jogo participation model.

A. Situational Leadership Theory

Probably the most popular leadership model, and the one most frequently applied in leadership development and training, was originally developed by consulting and training

Gurs Paul Hersey and Ken Blanchard as the "life cycle theory of leadership". It evolved through several versions into the situational leadership theory, the promise of which is that a leader's style should be contingent on subordinates competence and commitment.

Situational leadership theorists attempt to determine the appropriate leadership style for various situations. Several concepts which are important to understand situational leadership theory are:

(i) **Direction behaviours**: These involve telling a subordinate the how, what, when, and where of a task and closely supervising task accomplishment.

(ii) **Supportive behaviours**: These entail listening to subordinates, supporting and encouraging their progress, and involving them in decision making.

(iii) **Development level**: This refers to subordinate's competence in setting and attaining goals related to a specific task and commitment to accepting responsibility for those goals.

According to situational leadership theory, managers assess an employee's development level on a continuum, such as the one move up to the part of curved line above the development level to ascertain the appropriate levels of directive and supportive behaviours—that is, the leadership style.

Employee at position D_1 on the continuum are high in commitment, but low in competence, D_2 are moderate in competence and low in commitment. D_2 the manager must employ a directing leadership style (S1) For D2 employees the manager must employ coaching leadership style 52 (High level of direction). For D3 the manager has to employ supporting leadership style S3. For D4 employees are both fully competent and fully committed. For these employees delegating leadership style (S4) is appropriate, allowing the subordinates full rein to determine how to perform their task

Application of the situational leadership model is not easy. Managers must first observe and communicate with employees to determine their level of development Managers must also be flexible in applying direction and support because employees vary from one another, as wells as with in themselves, over time and from task to task. Moreover, employees may not initially agree with a managers assessment of their development level, thus requiring a leader's skill in arriving at assessment censuses and an agreed upon leadership style, a process called contracting for leadership style.

B. Fielder's Contingency Theory

The contingency leadership model is used to determine if one's leadership style is task oriented or relationship oriented and if the situation matches the leader's style. The successful leadership requires matching leaders with primarily stable leadership styles to the demands of the situation.

Leadership Style: The first major factor is to determine one's leadership style as being task or relationship oriented. To do so, the leader fills in the least preferred coworker (LPC) scales. The LPC essentially answers the questions. Are you more task oriented or people relationship oriented in working with others.

Situational Favorableness: Situational favorableness refers to the degree a situation enables the leader to exert influence over the followers. Three variables, in order of importance, are:

(i) **Leader -member relations:** The extent to which the leader is accepted by group members and has their support, respect, and good will is the most important determinant of favorability.

(ii) **Task Structure:** The degree to which a task is well defined or has standard procedures for goal accomplishment. Creative and ambiguous tasks would be less structured.

(iii) **Position Power:** The extent to which a leader has formal authority over employees to evaluate their work, assign tasks, and administrator rewards, and punishment. By combining these three Situational variables, we can derive eight different situations called octants.

Style Effectivenes: Fiedler found that task oriented leaders tended to be most effective in the three most favorable and the least favorable situations (octants 1, 2, 3/8), while relationship oriented leaders were most effective in the situations of moderate favorableness (octants 4, 5, 6, 7) If the leader's style does not match the situational demands. Fielder would advise the leader to alter the situation, perhaps by restructuring the task or seeking more position power.

House's Path-Goal Model: The Path-Goal Theory proposed by Robert J. House[27] is an important landmark in the development of leadership theory. This model attempts to predict leadership effectiveness in different situations. The term Path-Goal is employed because the leader smooths the path work goals and provides reward for achieving them.[28] This theory focuses on how leader influence employees, perceptions of the valence, instrumentality and expectancy. This theory incorporates four major types of styles.[29]

The essence of the theory is that it is the leader's job to assist his or her followers in attaining their goals and to provide the necessary direction and/or support to ensure that their goals are compatible with the overall objectives of the group or organization. The term "path-goal" is derived from the belief that effective leaders clarify the path to help their followers get from where they are to the achievement of their work goals and make the journey along the path easier by reducing roadblocks and pitfalls. (Ribbions, p. 380).

According to path-goal theory, a leader's behaviour is acceptable to subordinate to the degree that they view it as an immediate source of satisfaction or as a means of future satisfaction. A leader's behaviour is motivational to the degree that it (i) makes subordinate and need satisfaction contingent on effective performance; and (ii) provides the counseling, guidance, support and rewards that are necessary for effective performance. To test these statements, House identified four leadership behaviours.

(a) **Directive leadership:** This style is similar to that of the Lippitt and White authoritarian leader. Subordinates know exactly what is expected of them, and specific directions are given by the leader. There is no participation by subordinates.

(b) **Supportive leadership:** The leader is friendly and approachable and shows a genuine concern for subordinates.

(c) **Participative leadership:** The leader asks for and uses suggestions from subordinates but still makes the decisions. And

(d) **Achievement-oriented leadership:** The leader sets challenging goals for subordinates and shows confidence that they will attain these goals and perform well.

In contrast to fielder's view of a leader's behaviour, House assumes that leaders are flexible. Path-goal theory implies that the same leader can display any or all of those behaviours depending on the situation.

Path-goal theory proposes two classes of situations or contingency variables that moderate the leadership behaviour outcome relationship-those in the environment that are outside the control of the subordinate (task structure, the formal authority system, and the work group) and those that are a part of the personal characteristics of the subordinate (locus of control, experience, and perceived ability) environmental factors determine the type of leader behaviour required as a complement of subordinate outcomes are to be maximized, while personal characteristics of the subordinate determine how the environment and leader behaviour are interpreted. So the theory proposes that leader behaviour will be ineffective when it is redundant with sources of environmental structure or incongruent with subordinate characteristics.

Hersey and Blanchard presented a form of situational leadership based on the "readiness" level of the people the leader is attempting to influence. Readiness is the extent to which followers have the ability and willingness to accomplish a specific task. It is not a personal characteristic of the individual, but how ready the individual is to perform a particular task. Readiness is divided into a continuum of four levels; RI (Low), R2 and R3 (moderate), R4 (high)

- Rl-Low follower readiness-refers to followers who are both unable and unwilling, and who lack commitment and motivation; or who are unable and insecure.
- R2-Low to moderate followers readiness—referes to followers who are unable but willing, and who lack ability to perform but are unwilling to apply their ability; or who are able but insecure.
- R3-Moderate to high follower readiness—refers to followers who are able but unwilling, and who have the ability and commitment to perform but

are unwilling to apply their ability; or who are able but insecure.

- R4-high follower readiness—refers to followers who are both able and willing, and who have the ability and commitment to perform; or who are able and confident.

For each of the four levels of maturity, the appropriate style or leadership is a communication of task behaviour and relationship behaviour.

- Task behaviour—is the extent to which the leader provides directions for the actions of followers, sets goals for them, and defines their roles and how to undertake them.
- Relationship behaviour—is the extent to which the leader engages in two-way communication with followers, listens to them, and provides support and encouragement.

From the combination of task behaviour and relationship behaviour derive four leadership styles: telling (S1) selling (S2) participating (S3) and delegation (S4). The appropriate leadership style corresponds with the readiness of the followers.

S1-Telling-emphasizes high amounts of guidance (Task behaviour) but limited supportive (relationship) behaviour. This style is most appropriate for low follower readiness (Rl).

S2- Selling-emphasis high amounts of both directive (task) and relationship behaviours. This style is most appropriate for low to moderate follower readiness. (R2)

S3-Participation-emphasizes high amounts of two-way communication and supportive (relationship) behaviour but low amounts of guidance (task behaviour). This style is most appropriate for moderate to high follower readiness (R3).

S4-Delegation-emphaszes little direction or support with low levels of both task and relationship behaviours. This style is most appropriate for high follower readiness. (R4)

Vroom - Jago Contingency Model

This model is provided initially by Victor Vroom and Philip Yetton; and latter revised and developed by Victor Vroom and Arthur Jago. This model is based on two aspects of a leaders decision: its quality and acceptance.

Decision Quality - or rationality is the effect that the decision has on group performance.

Decision acceptance - refers to the motivation and commitment of group members in implementing the decision.

The Vroom and Yetton's Model. The most recent edition to the contingency approach is the leadership participation model proposed by Victor Vroom and Philip Yetton.[30]

Victor Vroom and Phillip Yetton have researched leadership style in the context of how much participation the leader should allow subordinates in making decisions.[31] They identified and described five alternative decision styles that may be adopted by a leader. These five decision styles are summarized in the Table 3 below.

TABLE 3

The Five Alternative Decision
Style of the Vroom-Yetton Model

A-I.	Leader solves the problem or make the decision himself using the information available to him at the present time.
A-II.	Leader obtains any necessary information from subordinates, then decides on a solution to the problem

himself. Leader may or may not tell subordinates the purpose of his questions or give information about the problem or decision that leader working on. The input provided by them is clearly in response to his request for specific information. They do not play a role in the definition of the problem or in generating or evaluating alternative solutions.

C-I. Leader shares the problem with the relevant subordinates individually, getting their ideas and suggestions without bringing them together as a group. The leader makes the decision. This decision may or may not reflect his subordinates' influence.

C-I. Leader shares the problem with his subordinates in a group meeting. In this meeting leader obtains their ideas and suggestions. Then he makes the decision which may or may not reflect his subordinates' influence.

C-II Leader shares the problem with his subordinates as a group. Together they generate an evaluate alternatives and attempt to reach agreement (consensus) on a solution. His role is much like that of Chairman, coordinating the discussion, keeping it focused on the problem and making sure that the critical issues are discussed. He can provide the group with information.

Source: On the validity of the Vroom-Yetton model" but V.H. Vroom & A.g. Jago, *Journal of Applied Psychology*, 1978, Volume 63, pp. 151-162. Copyright © 1978 by the American Psychological Association.

Style AI and AII involve an autocratic decision styles as the leader does not tell subordinates what problems that he is dealing with. Style CI and CII involve consultative style as the leader consults subordinates by sharing the problem with them and asking their opinion. However, in both the autocratic and consultative styles the leader makes the final decision alone. In the fifth style i.e., Gil the leader adopts a group consensus approach to decision making and shares responsibility as well as authority with the entire group to arrive at a decision.

Over all, the more frequently observed successful styles are CII and GIL This model is a better predictor of decision acceptance than it is of decision quality.

Life Cycle Theory : Theory of Paul Hersey and Kenneth Blanchard[32] reflects systematic conceptualization of situational factors as related to leadership behaviour. It is based on curvilinear relationship[33] between task and relationships and maturity of followers. Hence, it is based on an inter-play among three variables-task behaviour, relationship-behaviour and the maturity of the followers.

Comparison of the Four Situational Approaches to Leadership

Approach	Leader Behaviour/ Styles	Situational factors	Outcome criteria
Fiedler's Contingency male	Task oriented (Low LPC) Relationship oriented (High LPC)	Task structure Leader member relations	Groups effectiveness
Vroom-Jago	Autocratic Consultative Group	— Quality of division — Information requirement — Problems structure — Follower's acceptance decision — Mutually of follower organizational goals	— Quality of division — Acceptance of decision by followers — Time to make division — Level of follower conflict
Path-goal	Directive Supportive Participative Achievement oriented	Follower characteristic Environmental factors	— Satisfaction — Payment

Hersey & Blanchard	Telling Selling	Task behaviour Relationship Participation Delegation	— High follower readiness behaviour

Source: Partly adapted from Ivanchevich and Matteson, p. 403.

Social learning theory can provide a model for the continuous and reciprocal interaction between the leader (including his or her congnitions) followers and macro-variables and the behaviour itself.[34] It seems to be comprehensive and viable theoretical foundation for understanding leadership. Although work has been done on the theoretical development of social learning approach to leadership, research applications are just getting underway. Only time will tell whether it will hold up as a viable reasonable approach to leadership or not.

REFERENCES

1. Robbins P. Stephen, *Organizational Behaviour*, 2nd edition, Prentice-Hall of India (P) Ltd., New Delhi, 1985, p. 286.
2. Luthans, Fred, *Organizational Behaviour*, 4th edition, McGraw-Hill Book Company, New York, p. 479.
3. Stogdill. R.M.. *op. cit.*, 1974. p. 17-23.
4. Ghiseli. Edwine, *Explorations in Management Talent*. Pacific Palisades. Publications, 1971. pp. 122-130.
5. Davis, Keith, *op. cit.*, pp. 39-82.
6. Vroom, V.H. *The Search for a Theory of Leadership*. Englewood Cliffs Prentice-Hall, 1974. p. 397.
7. Davis Keith, *Human Behaviour at Work*, New York McGraw-Hill Book Company, 1981, pp. 124-125.
8. James. Owens, *The Use of Leadership Theory*, Prentice-Hall Inc. 1983 p. 42.
9. Terry, G.r. & Franklin, S.G., *Principles of Management*, 8th edition, All India Traveler Book Seller, New Delhi, 1984, p. 331.
10. Lewin K. Lippitt, R and White, R.K., *op. cit.*, 1939.
11. Stogdll R.M. and Coons, *op. cit.*, 1957.
12. Katz, Macoby and Morse, *op. cit.*, 1950.
13. Terry Franklin, *op. cit.*, 1984, pp. 332-333.

14. Fleishman, Edwin A., The Leadership Opinion Questionnaire, In Leader Behaviour and its Description and Measurement. Stogdill, R.M., and Coons S, A.E., (Columbus Bureau of Business Research Ohio State University, 1957).
15. Robbins, S.P., *op. cit.*, p. 289.
16. Yulk, G.A., *Toward A Behavioural Theory of Leadership, Organization Behaviour and Human Performance*, 1971.
17. Stogdill, R.M., *op. cit.*, 1974, pp. 17-23.
18. Daniel, C. et al, *op. cit.*, p. 297.
19. Luthans Fred, *op. cit.*, 1985, p. 476.
20. Daniel, C.K. et. al, *op. cit.*, p. 298.
21. Katz, Maccoby and Morse, *op. cit.*, 1950.
22. James L. Gibson, Jahn M. Ivancewishi and James A. Donally, Organisation, Business Publications Texas, 1979, p. 208.
23. Miner B. John., *The Uncertain Future of the Leadership Concept: An overview*, in James G. Hund and Larson. L. (eds) Kent State University, *Comparative Administration* Resources Institute, Kent, Ohio, 1975, pp. 197-208.
24. Tannenbaum, Robert and Warren H. Schmidt, *op. cit.*, pp. 95-101.
25. Tannenbaum, Robert and Warren H. Schmidt, *op. cit.*, pp. 95-101.
26. Fielder, F.E., *A Theory of Leadership Effectiveness*, McGraw - Hill Book, Company New York, 1967, pp. 13-144.
27. House Reober J., *op. cit.*, 1971, pp. 321-328.
28. Viroom, V. *Work and Motivation*, John Wiley and Sons, New York , 1964.
29. House Rober J, and Terence R. Mitchell., "Path-Goal Theory of Leadership," *Journal of Contemporary Business*, Autumn, 1974, pp. 81 -97.
30. Victor H. Vroom and Philip W. yetton, *op. cit.*, pp. 1-50.
31. Victor H. Vroom and Phillip W. Yetton, *Ibid.*
33. Korman, A.K., Consideration and Initiating Structure an Organizational Criteria, A Review, Personal psychology, *A Journal of Applied Research*, XIX, No. 4, Winter, 1966, pp. 349-361.
34. Davis, R.V. and Luthas Fred, A Social Learning Approach to organizational Behaviour, *Academy of Management Review*, April, 1980, pp. 281-290.

4

LEADERSHIP STYLES : A CONCEPTUAL APPROACH

The concept of leadership style has widely accepted and used by many management scientists, psychologists and even by social scientists. Leadership style has been defined by them according to their logic and philosophy, for example, McGregor (1967)[1] defines 'Style' as a method of coping with organizational reality, which evolves out of trail and error and is not deliberately adopted or eventually recognized by the leader. The predictable ways of coping with the reality of the work environment, according to him, may be as managerial styles. Hersey and Blanchard (1982)[2] view leadership styles of an individual as the behaviour pattern that a person exhibits when attempting to influence the activities of others as perceived by those others.

Keith Davis[3] states that "Leadership is practised by the leadership style, which is the total pattern of leader's action in relation to followers. It represents their philosophy, skill and attitudes in practice".

Types of Leadership Style

The customary approach to the analysis of leader behaviour is to classify various types of leadership into styles. The style is the way in which the leader influences followers. The styles are based on types of control leaders exercise in a group and their behaviour toward group members. The styles vary o I, the basis of the duties the leader feels he alone should perform; the responsibilities the leader expects his followers to accept; and the philosophical commitment of the leader to the development and fulfillment of subordinate's expectations. It also varies with the occasion, as well as with the types of leaders and followers. Most important is that effective leaders alter their own styles to fit the needs of a particular situation.

Autocratic or Authoritarian Leadership

An autocratic leader is work-centered or leader- centered. He concentrates all the authority and all the decision-making powers in himself. He structures the complete work situation for his employees. There is no participation by his subordinates in the decision-making process; they simply do what they are told to do. He tolerates no deviation from the orders. His subordinates fully depend upon him and are unaware of the goals of the organization. The leader takes and assumes full responsibility for decision making, for initiating action, and for directing, motivating and controlling his subordinates.

This is because the autocratic leader may think that he is the only competent and capable individual, and that his subordinates are incapable or unwilling to guide themselves, or he may have other reasons for assuming a strong position of guidance and control. The response, expected from the subordinates is obedience and adherence to his decisions. The style can be "soft sell", but it is usually perceived as "hard sell" -in either case, subordinates are permitted little freedom. The leader usually says:

> "Look, I am the boss around here. I'll make the decisions and I'll tell you what I want you to do. You would better do your job because I will be watching your every move."

Persons who employ autocratic or authoritarian styles of leadership could be termed "tellers". In order to be successful, such person must have a broad and diversified background.[4]

Autocratic style is efficient; needs little or no time to consult others during the decision making process; and it works well in developed situations when decision must be made and acted on quickly and without question. But employees often resent and resist leadership that excludes them from any involvement. Since autocratic communication is essentially one way, the resulting lack of feedback can lead to misunderstanding and subsequent mistakes. Making decisions without first listening to the advice of others can result in poor decisions. Finally, this type of leadership is usually negative because the followers are generally ill-informed, unsecured and afraid of the leaders' authority. Individual growth is far more difficult to attain within an autocratic framework; and it may fail to develop the workers' commitment to the objectives of the organization.

However, autocratic style might be used during an emergency occasioned by the breakdown of machinery with which the manager is familiar or when fire breaks out and there is a danger of the property and building being completely engulfed by it.

Under the umbrella of autocratic leadership, there are two different styles; the tough autocrat and the benevolent autocrat. Whatever the type, the autocratic leader believes that his leadership is based on the authority conferred on him by his position. He usually fells that this position of power automatically constrains his followers to obey his order and follow his instructions unquestioningly.

The tough autocrat views leadership as a matter of issuing orders. His followers must obey them unquestioningly. Often, such leadership generates a sense of insecurity and a lack of confidence in the employees which, in turn, necessitate their close supervision and swift punishment for any failure to perform a task as directed. The motto of a tough autocrat is: "Pay for performance, and praise sparingly." He relies on money as a sufficient reward and its deprivation as a punishment or as an instrument for changing their behaviour.

Main Characteristics of a Tough Autocrat are:

He makes all the decisions;

(a) He right to lad is derived from his positional authority;

(b) He rewards with wage increase and praise; and punishes by imposing penalties;

(c) Often, he conceals information from his followers in order to maintain his position as the fountain source of all knowledge; and

(d) He describes each job in detail and imposes rigid work standards on his employees.

His Employees' Emotional Reactions to Him are:

(a) Resentment of the leader and his methods;

(b) Resistance to his orders;

(c) Fear and dependence;

(d) Frustration flowing from a lack of opportunity to demonstrate their ability and perform actions without prior approval and constant supervision, and

(e) Security gained from the knowledge that their acceptance by the autocrat is earned, by them when they follow orders.

The Tough Autocrat Leadership is Useful When:

(a) Subordinates are new on a job and have had no experience;

(b) In an emergency, when decisions must be taken immediately;

(c) When a work group becomes complacent and needs to be goaded into action; and

(d) When disciplinary action is called for and when hostility and aggressiveness are to be dealt with effectively.

Situation in Which this Type of Leadership is Not Desirable are:

(a) When employees are knowledgeable about their jobs and have a considerable experience with the tasks they are called upon to perform;

(b) When an established and successful work group has already been formed and is successfully working to realize its objectives;

(c) When a job calls for team work and co-operation among employees; and

(d) When the supervisor is interested in improving morale and group attitudes towards the management.

This style of leadership gets results, but its consequences are not desirable. Subordinates lose interest and initiative, and depend entirely upon the boss's instructions. They become "yes men," frustrated, they lose confidence, and hardly acquire any managerial ability.[5]

The benevolent autocrat, on the other hand, is often referred to as a paternalistic leader. He looks upon himself as a parent figure. He praises his employees for work well done, and encourages them and even demands that they consult him for the solution of their problems. Father knows best -this attitude best describes this type of leader. He tries to create a climate in which employees cannot take any action without his prior approval. He is the dispenser of knowledge and approval; and he takes pride in the control of all the actions and in the accomplishments of his subordinates. Every act of his subordinates is evaluated in terms of their agreement with the thinking and wishes of their boss. Loyalty on their part is highly valued by the leader. Initiative, change and independent action are not permitted to them because they are the prerogatives of the leader.

The chief characteristics of a benevolent autocrat are:

(a) He stifles the creativity and innovative ability of his subordinates, resents those who are disloyal to him or who openly display a positive attitude to change;

(b) He takes all the decisions;

(c) He is concerned with the details of a job, tends to play the role of an all-knowing person, and is the fountain source of all information for his subordinates.

The Emotional Reactions of Subordinates to Such Leadership Are:

(a) Frustration arising out of their inability to work without supervision;

(b) Disrespect towards the boss, which is shown in the guise of friendship or outward show of respect;

(c) Dependence on his attention to the family details of the subordinates; and

(d) An atmosphere of trust, often felt by members of the group, though they do not necessarily respect the superior or his actions.

The Benevolent Autocrat is Useful When

(a) his subordinates are not interested in seeking responsibility;

(b) when they enjoy a strong and friendly leadership; and

(c) when they are immature and must be closely supervised.

However, this style of leadership is unhelpful when (i) it comes to dealing with strong; independent and mature employees who want to participate in the decision-making processes of their group, and (ii) when it is essential to build up a cadre of leaders for the future.

Consultative, or Participative, or Democratic, or Group-Centered Leadership

This type of leadership centralizes managerial authority. The leader's decisions are taken after consultation with his followers and after their participation in the decision-making process He involves the members of his group in the decisions on the feasibility and workability of an idea, or a job and its content, and on the extent and the content of the problems that affect them. He believes that their cooperation in the attainment of organizational goals can be enlisted only if they are committed to the organization, and that commitment can be ensured only by an honest and open communication of ideas with them and by the development of a team spirit He encourages his subordinates to function as a social unit, and makes full use of their talents and abilities. "He is the conductor of an orchestra rather than a one-man band; and he realizes that this job is to co-ordinate the willing work of his employees".

Participative Leaders call for subordinates to exercise high degrees of both responsibility and freedom. They use as little authoritarian control as possible, and are concerned with group relationship as well as getting the job done. They do not delegate their right to make final decisions and to give specific directives to their subordinates, but to seek their thoughts and opinions on many decisions that affect them. Such leaders cultivate the decision-making abilities of their subordinates and encourage to increase their abilities to exercise self-control and urge them to assume greater responsibility for guiding their own efforts.[6]

Participative style is very useful in many ways. When workers feel their ideas are important and being made use of, they feel considerably committed to change in which they have participated. Workers also develop a greater feeling of self-esteem. They maximize their potential in creative and productive ways and experience personal satisfaction and accomplishment of their tasks. Further, when most people are given a little freedom, they develop and grow personality and in job competence: Often they will take on more responsibility then their job descriptions call for because of the pleasure they take in their work.

On the other hand, participative leadership can be very time consuming and requires a great deal of energy. Sometimes participation can mean that little or no planning gets done at all, which can result in situations getting out of control. People can use participation with authority as a guise for shirking their own responsibilities and as a way to pass the buck to others. Another potential problem with the participation is that group members whose ideas have been rejected may feel alienated.

The participative leader adopts a helpful attitude toward his subordinates. He often says: "I am sure you understand that the final responsibility for making a decision is mine, but you are most welcome to often your suggestions and give ideas and feelings. I will help you in the implementation of the decision once it has been made."

There are two types of participative leaders viz.: democratic leaders and consultative leaders Democratic leaders are those who confer final authority to the group; they abide by whatever the group decides. A democratic leadership involves group discussions and decisions on policy on the basis of the technical advice supplied by the leader; it involves a free choice of work partners, and "objective" praise and criticism by the leader. Consultative leaders are those who require a high degree of involvement from employees, but who make it clear that they alone have the authority to make final decisions.

The Chief Characteristics of Participative Leadership are:

(a) The leader delegates as much responsibility to the members of the work team as their experience and knowledge will permit;

(b) He places emphasis on results rather than on action. His philosophy is: "It is not always how a job gets done that is important but that the job does get done."

(c) He shows concern for his employees and thereby gains their respect;

(d) He encourages co-operation when it will lead to greater productivity and creativity;

(e) He defines the objectives for the group and gives its members some freedom for performance within the standards laid down by him and;

(f) He takes all the decisions and accepts full responsibility.

The emotional reactions of his subordinates to this style of leadership are: (a) A feeling of cooperation with boss; (b)

Respect for him as a person; (c) Warm and friendly relations between superior and subordinates; (d) Greater motivation and higher morale; and (e) Better formulation of plans and better decisions because of discussions and the pooling of experience.

However, this style of leadership is the least effective when: (a) Employees lack experience and training and (b) There are groups in which employees do not wish to work as a team; or when they are unable to do so because of the nature of the work or the geographical distance between employees.

Participative style of leadership is more appropriate under conditions in which: (i) the company has communicated its goals and objectives to the subordinates and subordinates have accepted them; (ii) where the company practices use rewards and involvement as the primary means of motivation and control; (iii) where the leader-supervisor truly desires to hear the ideas of other before making decisions; (iv) where the leader wishes to develop analytical and self-control abilities in the subordinates; (v) where the workers are reasonably knowledgeable and experienced; (vi) where subordinates desire involvement in matters that affect them; (vii) where the group has a proven record of cooperation and performance; and (viii) workers are able to work independently with little or no direct contact with the supervisor.

Free-Rein or Laissez Faire or Group-Centred Leadership

This is often described "as no leadership at all", for there is the absence of direct leadership. Under this style, the leader delegates the authority for decision-making into the hands of the subordinates rather completely. A task is ordinarily presented to the group, which establishes its own goals and works out its own techniques for accomplishing those goals within the framework of organizational policy. The leader in effect says to his followers:

> "Here is a job for you to do. Do it any way you want to so long it gets done. I will only expect to hear from you when you are experiencing unusually difficult problems".

The leader expects his subordinates to assume responsibility for their own motivation, guidance, and control. Except for the stating of a minimum member of ground rules, leader provides very little guidance and support for the followers. He acts principally as a liaison between outside sources and the group and ascertains that necessary resource are available to the group.[7]

Discipline and control are not enforced in the hope that employees will themselves enforce them, whenever necessary The free-rein leader believes that one who leads the least leads best.

The behaviour of the leader in the laissez-fair style of leadership involves little direction; there is complete group of individual freedom in decision-making, and no appraisal or regulation of the performance of the subordinates is made.

The Main Characteristics of Such Leadership are:

(a) Maximum concern for the individuals who make up the work team;

(b) Open discussions and creativity, and respect for all views; and

(c) The majority will is operative in the decision-making process.

The Emotional Reactions of the Followers to this Style of Leadership are:

(a) A free and informal work environment, in which each individual can seek his answers to the problems posed by his job;

(b) Insecurity and frequent frustration because of want of specific decision-making authority and responsibility;

(c) Lack of cohesive behaviour; cliques are often formed to the detriment of the group's goal-directed action.

This pattern of leadership suffers from some drawbacks. For example: (a) The work group generally has some members who refuse to cooperate; (b) It is unable or unwilling to reach a decision; (c) It is either too large to work effectively, or it lack necessary cohesion which may enable it to arrive at a decision; and (d) in some instances it could degenerate into chaos.

The Free-Rein Style of Leadership Would be Most Effective:

(i) under companies where its goals and the subordinates' goals are highly compatible; and they have been thoroughly communicated and are acceptable to the subordinates;

(ii) when the leader desires to delegate decision-making fully;

(iii) when the leader has a high degree of confidence in the abilities of his subordinates;

(iv) when the subordinates themselves are well-trained and highly knowledgeable concerning their jobs and are willing to assume responsibility for decision-making and self-control;

(v) when the subordinates have a high need for independence;

(vi) when the subordinates derive large personal satisfaction from their work; and

(vii) where performance demands allow some room for error if mistakes occur in rather decentralized arrangement.

To some degree free-rein leadership is found among certain professional workers such as university professors, route salesmen, engineers, scientists, as there is a limited amount of supervision on people in these areas.

Besides there three main styles, there are others too.

Bureaucratic or Rules-Centred Leadership: The leader's behaviour is characterized by a high degree of reliance on rules, regulations and procedures, to which both he and his subordinates subscribe. As a result, the process of administration is reduced to a series of routine actions. The rules specify the obligations of the subordinates, and enjoin upon them to do particular things in specific ways. There is no participation or initiative on their part. This style of leadership fosters worker apathy. The rules serve as a specification of the minimum level of acceptable performance. It is possible for workers to remain apathetic, for they know just how little they should do to remain secure in their jobs. This leads to what is called bureaucratic sabotage-a deliberate apathy fused with resentment so that every act of conforming to the letter of the rule is accompanied by a conscious intention to violate it. Rules make it possible for workers to indulge in activity without participation; they enable them to work without being emotionally committed to work. Rules also lead to red tape and the habit of passing the buck, too much paper work and too great a desire to play safe.[8]

Manipulative Leadership

This style of leadership is based on the belief that employees are persons who should be manipulated by the leader so that his goal may be attained. It exploits the aspirations of the employees. Under this style of leadership, employees know that they are being manipulated, and, therefore, become resentful and bitter. A manipulative leader, however, is very sensitive about the needs and desires of his employees as individuals. But the information gathered as a result of this sensitivity is not used for the benefit of the employees; instead, it is utilized by him for his own personal profit.

The main characteristics of this style of leadership are: (a) Personal goals are reached by a manipulation of the employees; (b) Employee needs and desires are viewed as tools to extract performance.

The emotional reactions of the subordinates to this style of leadership are: (a) A highly motivated work group, believing that it has found a manager who understands its needs, and will help it realize those needs; (b) A distrust arises when the manipulative nature of the leader becomes evident, and the employees discover that they have been duped.

But this style of leadership is effective only in specific situations; for example, when co- operation and co-ordination have to be achieved on a project and previous leaders were unable to motivate the group properly; or when highly motivated employees are needed for short -duration projects. They are often given the illusion of reward, and are thus motivated for short periods.

However, manipulative leadership is not effective when: (i) A relationship of long-standing is involved; and (ii) The structure of an open.

Factors Affecting Choice of Leadership

As a manager works with his organization, his choice of a leaders is governed by certain forces, These are:

(i) Forces acting on the manager;
(ii) Forces acting on the subordinates; and
(iii) Forces acting on the situation.

(i) *Forces Acting on the Manager*: In any given situation, the behaviour of the manager is influenced by his own personality; that basis of his background, knowledge and experience. The important forces affecting him are :

(a) His value system; that is, the relative importance he attaches to organizational efficiency, the personal growth of his subordinates, and company profits.

(b) His confidence in his subordinates, which is influenced by the knowledge and competence they have.

(c) His own leadership inclination; that is, whether he can function comfortably land naturally or whether he is uncomfortable when operating in a team.

(d) His feeling of security in an uncertain situation. In other words his tolerance of ambiguity is taken as an important variable in his dealing with problems.

(ii) *Forces Acting on the Subordinates*: The leader needs a knowledge of the factors which influence his employees' personality. The manager may grant greater freedom to his subordinate if he is assured that:

(a) The subordinate has a relatively high need for independence;

(b) He is ready to assume responsibility for decisions;

(c) He is interested in the problem which is important;

(d) He has a relatively high tolerance of ambiguity;

(e) He understands, and identifies himself with, the goals of the organization;

(f) He has the necessary knowledge and experience to deal with problems; and

(g) He has learnt to expect that he would share in the decision making process.

(iii) *Forces Acting on the Situation*: Some aspects of a general situation affect the manager's behaviour. These are:

(a) The type of organization for which he works, its values and traditions which are communicated through job description, policy announcements and public statements by top executives.

(b) The qualities of the leader. Some organizations require that their executives should be dynamic, imaginative, decisive, persuasive, while other place emphasis on their ability to work effectively with people.

(c) The size of a working unit, its geographical location, and the extent of inter-and intra-organizational security which is needed to attain company goals-these also affect the quality and extent of employee participation.

(d) Group effectiveness, i.e., the leader should know that a group which has a long standing is in the habit of working in cooperation. Moreover, the confidence which members of a group have in their ability to solve a problem as a group is also to be borne in mind. Cohesiveness, permissiveness, mutual acceptance and a common purpose also influence the functioning of a group.

(e) The nature of the problem itself may determine

whether authority should be delegated to subordinates, and, if so, to what extent.

(f) The pressure of time when this pressure is intense, decisions have to be taken quickly with a high degree of authority. If this is not possible, subordinates may be given a share in the decision-making process.[9]

REFERENCES

1 McGregor, Dougal., *op. cit.*, 1967, p. 58

2 Paul Hersey and Blanchard, K.H., *op. cit.* 1982, p. 233.

3 Devis, Keith, *op. cit.*

4. I Nelson, Debrab and Quick, James Campbell, *Organizational Behaviour: Foundations, Realities and Challenges* New York. 1997. p. 389.

5. Debra Nelson et al., *op. cit.* p. 356.

6. *Ibid.*, pp. 356-358.

7. *Ibid.*, pp. 359-360.

8. *Ibid.*, p. 370.

9. Francis, G. James and Milbourn, Gene, *Human Behaviour in the Work Environment: A Management Perspective,* Santa Monica, Goodyear Publishing Company, Inc. 1980, pp. 65-66.

5

PERSONAL BACKGROUND OF LEADERS (OWNER-MANAGERS) IN SMALL SCALE INDUSTRIES—A SURVEY ANALYSIS

The results of this study are based on a sample of sixty owner-managers owing small scale industries in Nellore town. Their personal data have been outlined as under:

Proprietorship Category-wise Classification of Owner-Managers

Particulars of this aspect are furnished below:

TABLE 1

Distribution of Owner-Managers as per Proprietorship

(N=60)

Ownership Category	*Number of Units*	*Percentage to Total*
Sole traders	51	85
Partnership	9	15
Total	60	100

Source: Field Survey.

Of the total sample of sixty units selected, 85 per cent is accounted by sole trading concerns and the remaining 15 per cent by partnership firms. The domination of sole trading concerns in the total number of business units in the universe also holds good in the study under reference.

Sex Wise Classification of Owner-Managers

Sample owner-managers in the succeeding table are classified according to their sex.

TABLE 2

Sex Wise Classification of Owner-Managers

N = 60

Sex	*Owner-Manager*			
	Sole Trader		*Partnership*	
	Number	*Percentage to Total*	*Number*	*Percentage to Total*
Male	49	96.07	9	100
Female	2	3.93	—	—
Total	51	100.00	9	100

Source: Field Survey.

It is obvious from the table above that female participation in case of soletrading business is insignificant being only 4 per cent and even this is not existent in the case of partnership which is very much discouraging.

Owner-Managers—Their Training

Sample owner-managers are classified according to trained and untrained and the results are furnished in the succeeding Table 3.

At present training is an important factor for the success of the management. Of the total sixty sample owner-managers, nearly 80 per cent are trained and the remaining are untrained. In the case of sole proprietorship the trained component is more than 90 per cent which is the basic ingredient for the success of sole proprietorship in arena of business unit in spite of the evaluation of various types of business organizations that are evidenced especially after the advent of Industrial revolution.

TABLE 3

Owner-Managers - Their Training

(*N* = 60)

Training	*Owner Managers*			
	Sole Trader		*Partnership*	
	Number	*Percentage to total*	*Number*	*Percentage to total*
Trained	47	92.16	7	77.77
Untrained	4	7.84	2	22.23
Total	51	100.00	9	100.00

Source: Field Survey.

Owner-Managers' Classification According to Their Mother-tongue

Mothertongue particulars of sample owner-managers are given in the ensuing table:

TABLE 4

Sample Owner-Managers—Their Mother-Tongue

(*N* = 60)

Mother tongue	*Owner Managers*			
	Sole Trader		*Partnership*	
	Number	*Percentage to total*	*Number*	*Percentage to total*
Telugu	35	68.63	5	56
Urdu	16	31.37	4	44
Total	51	100.00	9	100

Source: Field Survey.

Of the total sixty sample owner-managers 67 per cent are Telugu speaking managers and the remaining are Urdu speaking. Among the sole traders 69 per cent are Telugu speaking but this is some what lower in the case Partnership being only 56 percent. Though, Urdu speaking in the country accounted for only 10 per cent, the larger percentage of this category in Nellore Town may be attributed to the fact that most of Muslims are engaged in small business organizations.

Age-wise Classification of Owner-Managers

Particulars of Age-wise classification of owner-managers are furnished in Table below :

TABLE 5

Age-Wise Distribution of Owner-Managers

(N = 60)

Age Group	*Owner Managers*			
	Sole Trader		*Partnership*	
	Number	*Percentage to total*	*Number*	*Percentage to total*
20-25	2	3.92	1	11.11
25-30	10	19.61	1	11.11
30-35	13	25.49	4	44.44
35-40	10	19.61	2	22.22
40-45	5	9.80	—	—
45-50	5	9.80	1	11.11
50-55	1	1.96	—	—
55-60	2	3.92	—	—
60-65	2	3.92	—	—
65-70	—	—	—	—
70-75	1	1.97	—	—
Total	51	100.00	9	100.00

Source: Field Survey.

The particulars in the table above reveal that model age of owner-managers in the case of sole trading concerns as well as partnership firms is 35-40, whereas the average age in these cases workes out to 37.92 and 33.61 respectively.

Classification of Owner-Managers According to Education

Sample owner-manger are classified according to their level of education and the results are furnished in the succeeding table.

TABLE 6

Distribution of Owner-Managers According to Their Level of Education

(N = 60)

	Owner Managers			
	Sole Trader		*Partnership*	
Level of Education	*Number*	*Percentage to Total*	*Number*	*Percentage to Total*
S.S.C	17	39.53	—	—
Intermediate	15	34.88	2	22.22
Graduation	8	18.60	5	55.55
Post Graduation	—	—	—	—
Technical	3	6.98	2	22.23
Total	43	100.00	9	100.00

Source: Field survey.

The highest number of owner-managers in the case sole trading Concern are with SSC qualification being nearly 40 percent followed by those with intermediate qualification (about 35 percent), where as graduates account for more than half of the owner managers, in the case of partnership firms. But the noticeable factor in this case is that owner managers with technical qualification account only for a very meager percentage i.e. 7 per cent in case of sole trading concerns through it is 22 percent in case of partnership firms.

Family Background of Owner-Managers

Particulars of family background of owner-managers are furnished in the table below:

TABLE 7

Family Background- wise Distribution of Owner-Managers

(N = 60)

	Owner Managers			
	Sole Trader		*Partnership*	
Family Background	*Number*	*Percentage to total*	*Number*	*Percentage to total*
Agriculture	7	13.73	—	—
Business	34	66.67	4	44.44
Profession	10	19.60	5	55.56
Total	51	100.00	9	100.00

Source: Field Survey.

Owner-managers who hailed from agricultural background account for only 14 percent (approximate) in case of sole trading concerns while it is zero in case of partnership firms. Two-thirds of owner-managers in the case of sole trading concerns and 44 percent (approximate) in case partnership firms hail from business families, nearly 56 percent in case of partnership firms and 20 percent in case of sole trading concerns owner-managers are from professional families.

Family Type Classification of Owner-Managers

The family type particulars of sample owner-managers are given in the ensuing table:

TABLE 8

Classification of Owner-Managers According to the Family Type

(N = 60)

Family	Owner Managers			
	Sole Trader		Partnership	
	Number	Percentage to total	Number	Percentage to total
Independent	35	69	5	56
Joint Family	16	31	4	44
Total	51	100	9	100

Source: Field Survey.

Table above shows that 69 per cent of owner-managers in the case of sole trading concerns belongs to independent category of families and the remaining 31 per cent are from Joint families. 56 per cent of owner-managers in the category of Partnership firms have come from independent families. The remaining 44 per cent of owner-managers in this category belongs to joint family. This confirms with the universal phenomenon of the existence of comparatively large number of independent families.

Owner-Managers—Their Experience

Particulars of the owner-managers according to their years of experience are noted in the Table 9.

It can be observed from the particulars in the Table above that most of the owner-managers in the case of sole trading concerns have an experience of a minimum period of 5 to a maximum of 30 years, whereas the minimum experience is same in the case of partnership firm but the maximum is only 15 years. The model experience group is 5-10 years in case of sole trading concern while this is not possible to calculate in the case of partnership firms. The average experience is 12.29 in sole trading concerns and 7.5 in partnership firms.

TABLE 9

Distribution of Owner-Managers on the Basis of Experience

(N = 60)

	Owner Managers			
	Sole Trader		*Partnership*	
Years of Experience	*Number*	*Percentage to total*	*Number*	*Percentage to total*
0-5	5	10	3	34
5-10	20	39	3	33
10-15	12	24	3	33
15-20	5	10	—	—
20-25	4	7	—	—
25-30	5	10	—	—
Total	51	100	09	100

Source: Field Survey.

Religion-wise Classification of Owner-Managers

Religion-wise particulars of owner-managers are furnished in the table.

Hindus account for the lion's share in the total number of owner-managers in case of sole trading concerns followed by Muslims. Similar case can be observed in the case of Partnership firms. This can be attributed to the religious character of India. Christians account for only a very meager percentage of the sample owner-managers being 2 percent in case of sole trading concerns and for nil percentage in case of partnership firms.

TABLE 10

Religion-wise Classification of Owner-Managers

(N = 60)

	Owner Managers			
	Sole Trader		*Partnership*	
Religion	*Number*	*Percentage to total*	*Number*	*Percentage to total*
Hindu	34	67	5	56
Muslim	16	31	4	44
Christian	1	2	0	0
Total	51	100	9	100

Source: Field Survey.

Association with Childhood Friends of Owner-Managers

Particulars of the sample owner-managers according to their association ship with childhood friends are noted in the table below:

TABLE 11

Classification of Owner-Managers According to Associationship with Childhood Friends

(N = 60)

	Owner Managers			
	Sole Trader		*Partnership*	
Childhood	*Number*	*Percentage to total*	*Number*	*Percentage to total*
Associated	15	29	3	33
Not Associated	36	71	6	67
Total	51	100	9	100

Source: Field Survey.

Majority of the owner-managers i.e., 71 per cent in the case of sole trading concerns and 67 per cent in the case partnership firms are not associated with their childhood friends.

(xii) Owner-Manager's Membership in the Club

Membership in the club particulars of owner-managers are given in the following Table.

TABLE 12

Classification of Owner-Managers as Per the Members in Any Club

(N = 60)

	Owner Managers			
	Sole Trader		*Partnership*	
Membership	*Number*	*Percentage to Total*	*Number*	*Percentage to Total*
Member	12	24	2	23
Non-member	39	76	7	77
Total	51	100	9	100

Source: Field Survey.

Majority of the owner-managers in both the cases of sole trader and partnership are not members in any club (76 per cent in the case of sole traders and 77 per cent in case of partnership firms).

6

LEADERSHIP STYLES IN SMALL-SCALE INDUSTRIES: A SURVEY ANALYSIS

The participative type of management is not likely to be successful in India as the Indian scene is different from aboard. For instance, the Indian culture is not permissive for this as it is being highly authoritarian and also the caste system encourages the tendency for security and dependency. Besides, employment opportunities, in India are also relatively less. Under these circumstances, it can be said that the negative incentives of firing, lay-off and disciplinary action are more successful in India. However, it can be noted that while it may be true to a certain extent, the younger generation is more independent than were their parents. Already there has been a move to a large extent from emphasis on owner-managers to reliance on the professional manager whether he may be an owner or not. Such a manager is more interested in the results rather than from whom a suggestion emanate. A move towards participative management has already begun in enlighted Indian companies. Also no style of leadership is best suited under all these circumstances. The socio cultural environment and the organizational climate are the important ones among various factors responsible for this prevalence. It is, however, felt that the managers in India would have to become increasingly participative because of the rapidly changing political, social and cultural environment. Not only these but also the demographic characteristics of owner-managers like education, age, experience and family background influence the styles of the behaviour of the owner-managers.

In the light of the above discussion this chapter attempts to demonstrate the different styles of sample owner-managers assuming the owner-manager himself as the leader. Also the formulated hypothesis viz., leadership styles of owner-managers will vary with the type of decision, education, age, experience and family background is also tested in this chapter.

Testing of Formulated Hypothesis

According to the hypothesis that the owner-managers use different leadership styles depending upon the type of situations.

As explained in the third chapter, owner-manages are asked to indicate on the leadership continuum having five different styles in relation to each seventeen decision-making questionnaire, their responses are summarized and are noted in the Table 1.

From the summarized results in the Table 1 it can be observed that the sample owner-managers are adopting only four styles in tackling each of the seventeen decision situations. While deciding about the size, location and lay-out of plant (Question No. 2), for instance, the owner-managers used styles II 56.67 percentage times and the same is the case in deciding about the decision to hire machinery (Question No. 8). Contrary to this, when it is a matter of decision regarding method of production and decision to get a loan, the same manager used style II (Question No. 3 and 11 respectively) to the extent of only 31.67 percent. Similarly, coming to the average of the particular style in all the seventeen situations put together it varies from 13.53 percent in case of style IV to 40.29 percent in case of style II, followed by 32.45 percent in case of style I. Thus, average figure for style II is the highest

TABLE 1

Leadership Styles of Owner-Managers in Percentage of Times the Style is Used

(N = 60)

Situations	*Leadership Styles*					*Total*
	I	*II*	*III*	*IV*	*V*	
1.	46.67	41.67	3.33	8.33	—	100
2.	23.33	56.67	16.67	3.33	—	100
3.	31.67	31.66	25.00	11.67	—	100
4.	31.66	35.00	11.67	21.67	—	100
5.	36.67	40.00	10.00	13.33	—	100
6.	31.67	43.33	10.00	15.00	—	100
7.	31.67	38.33	15.00	15.00	—	100
8.	25.00	55.00	13.33	15.00	—	100
9.	36.67	35.00	20.00	6.67	—	100
10.	26.67	38.33	10.00	25.00	—	100
11.	36.67	31.67	16.67	15.00	—	100
12.	28.33	40.00	15.00	16.67	—	100
13.	36.67	41.67	8.33	13.33	—	100
14.	35.00	40.00	13.33	11.67	—	100
15.	26.67	36.67	16.67	20.00	—	100
16.	31.67	35.00	16.67	16.67	—	100
17.	35.00	45.00	11.67	8.33	—	100
Mean Percentage	32.45	40.29	13.73	13.53	–	100

Source: Field Survey.

and lowest in case of style IV. However, use of style V did not emanate from any one of the respondent. Of course, this may be true in case of small scale industries where the workers have no voice in decision-making. However, it may be sometimes possible if the owner-manager is not qualified technically, he may consult his employees regarding technical matters but the final authority rests with himself.

Thus, the above discussion clearly indicates that the owner-managers in small scale industry use various leadership styles depending upon the situations. Hence, the formulated hypothesis viz., owner-managers use different types of leadership styles depending on different situations is accepted.

In order to investigate whether leadership styles of owner-manager vary with the type of decision, the details of seventeen decision situations included in the "Decision-Making" questionnaire are categories into four group. They are:

(i) Decisions concerned with production matters,

(ii) Decisions concerned with technical matters,

(iii) Decisions concerned with financial matters, and

(iv) Decisions concerned with personnel matters.

The following tables summarise the findings of the investigation.

Leadership Styles of Owner-Managers Concerned with Production Matters

The details of styles adopted by the sample owner-managers regarding decisions about production matters are shown in the Table 2.

It is evident from the details furnished in the Table 2, that 41.00 percent of sample owner-manager on an average are adopted style II (i.e. owner-managers own-decision without detailed explanation to their workers). This indicates that with regard to production matters the owner-managers on an average are adopting style II. The mean percentage of style II and I put together comes to 75.00 percent of the owner-managers and thus, 34 of the sample owner-managers are adopting the autocratic style. However, only 13.33 percent of owner-managers on an average are adopting style III (i.e. the leader shares the problem with relevant subordinates)

TABLE 2

Leadership Styles of Owner-Managers Concerned with Production Matters

(N = 60)

Situations	*Styles Adopted*										
	I		*II*		*III*		*IV*		*V*		*Total*
	Number	*%to total*	*Number*	*%to total*	*Number*	*%to total*	*Number*	*%to total*	*Number*	*%to total*	
1. Relating to Volume of output	28	46.67	25	41.67	2	3.33	5	8.33	—	—	100
2. Size, location and lay-out of plant	14	23.33	34	56.67	10	16.67	2	3.33	—	—	100
3. Method of Production	19	31.67	19	31.67	15	25.00	7	11.67	—	—	100
4. Purchasing Practices and amount of inventory	19	31.67	21	35.00	7	11.67	13	21.67	—	—	100
5. Wage payment	22	36.67	24	40.00	6	10.00	8	13.33	—	—	100
Mean Percentages		34.00		41.00		13.33		11.67			100

Source: Field Survey.

and style IV by 11.67 percent (i.e. the leader shares the problem with subordinates as a group. Style V is not followed by a one of the sample owner-managers.

Leadership styles of owner-managers concerned with Technical Matters: The Particulars of the type of styles adopted by sample owner-managers in making decisions concerned with technical matters are given in the Table 3

The Table 3 reveals leadership styles adopted by the sample owner-managers relating to technical matter. Looking at the mean percentage of the styles adopted. Style II is adopted by 42.91 percent of owner-managers, style I by 31.25 percent style III by 14.58 percent and style IV by 11.25 percent. Style V is followed by the none of the owner-managers. Mean percentages of style II and I put together comes to 74.16 percent of the owner-managers and thus nearly % of the sample owner-managers are adopting the autocratic style in respect of mattersrelating to technical aspects.

Leadership styles of owner-managers concerned with Financial Matters. Leadership styles adopted by the sample owner-managers in respect of decisions concerned with financial matters are furnished in the table.

The proceeding table reveals the leadership styles adopted by owner-managers relating to Financial matters. Basing on the mean percentages of the styles adopted it can be said that 36.67 percent of owner-managers adopted style II 30.56 percent style I, 18.89 percent style IV and 13.89 percent style III. None of the owner-managers followed style V. Mean percentages of style II and I combined together constitute 67.23 percent and thus more than 2/3rds of the sample owner-managers adopting the autocratic style while making decisions relating to financial matters.

Leadership styles of owner-managers concerned with

TABLE 3

Leadership Styles of Owner-Managers Concerned with Technical Matters

(N = 60)

Situations	*Styles Adopted*										
	I		*II*		*III*		*IV*		*V*		*Total*
	Number	*%to total*	*Number*	*%to total*	*Number*	*%to total*	*Number*	*%to total*	*Number*	*%to total*	
6. Operating procedure	19	31.67	26	43.33	6	10.00	9	15.00	—	—	100
7. New equipment Style	19	31.67	23	38.33	9	15.00	9	15.00	—	—	100
8. Hire Machinery	15	25.00	33	55.00	8	13.33	4	6.67	—	—	100
9. Employ new Subordinate	22	36.67	21	35.00	12	20.00	5	8.33	—	—	100
Mean Percentages		31.25		42.91		14.58		11.25			100

Source: Field Survey.

TABLE 4

Leadership Styles of Owner-Managers Concerned with Financial Matters

(N = 60)

Situations	*Styles Adopted*										*Total*
	I		*II*		*III*		*IV*		*V*		
	Number	*%to total*	*Number*	*%to total*	*Number*	*%to total*	*Number*	*%to total*	*Number*	*%to total*	
10. New Purchase of Machine	16	26.67	23	38.33	6	10.00	15	25.00	—	—	100
11. Get a loan	22	36.67	19	31.67	10	16.67	9	15.00	—	—	100
12. Any other financial matter	17	28.33	24	40.00	9	15.00	10	16.67	—	—	100
Mean Percentages		30.56		36.67		13.89		18.89			100

Source: Field Survey.

Personnel Matters : with respect to decisions concerned with personnel matters, the styles are detailed in the Table 5.

The Table 5 reveals the leadership styles adopted by owner-managers pertaining to personnel matters. Looking at the mean percentages of the styles adopted, it can be said that 39.67 percent of owner-managers are adopting style II, 33.00 percent style 1, 14.00 percent style IV and 13.33 percent style III. The mean percentages of style II & I, put together constitutes 72.67 percent. Hence, nearly 3/4ths of the sample owner-managers are adopting the autocratic style at the time of making decisions relating to personnel matters.

Even question-wise analysis is made and difference in adoption of styles by the sample owner-managers can be observed. In case of question No. 1 (i.e., decision to volume of output), 46.67 percent of owner-managers are using style I and 41.67 percent style II. A lower percentage of response (3.33 and 8.33 percent) has been evidenced both in the III and IV styles.

As regards question number 2 (i.e., decision as to size, location and layout of plant, style II tops with the highest percentage (i.e., 56.67 percent). Style I, III and IV occupy the next order.

It is seen in question number 3 (i.e., decision as to methods of production), 31.67 percent of owner-managers are adopting style I, 31.66, 25.00 and 11.67 percent of the owner-managers are adopting styles II, III and IV respectively.

In case of question number 4 (i.e., decision as to purchasing practices and amount of inventory), 35.00 per cent of owner-managers are using style II followed by style I (31.66 per cent), style IV (21.67 percent) and style III (11.67 per cent).

The response to question 5 (i.e., decision as to methods of wage payment) show that 40.00 percent of owner-managers

TABLE 5

Leadership Styles of Owner-Managers Concerned with Personnel Matters

(N = 60)

Situations	Styles Adopted										
	I		II		III		IV		V		Total
	Number	%to total	Number	%to total	Number	%to total	Number	%to total	Number	%to total	
13. Promote or punish the worker	22	36.67	25	41.67	5	8.33	8	13.33	—	—	100
14. To take disciplinary action against employees	21	35.00	24	40.00	8	13.33	7	11.67	—	—	100
15. To assign a different job to worker	16	26.67	22	36.67	10	16.67	12	20.00	—	—	100
16. To remove the worker	19	31.67	21	35.00	10	16.67	10	16.67	—	—	100
17. To pay any compensation	21	35.00	27	45.00	7	11.67	5	8.33	—	—	100
Mean Percentages		33.00		39.67		13.33		14.00			100

Source: Field Survey.

have been using style II and 36.67 percent style 1,13.33 per cent style IV and 10.00 per cent style III.

As regards to question number 6 (i.e., decision as to change the operation procedure) style II tops with the highest percentage i.e., 43.33 percent, styles I, IV and III occupies the next order.

In case of question number 7 (i.e., decision as to purchase of any new equipment) 38.33 percent of owner-managers are using style II and 31.67 percent style I. An equal percentage i.e., 15.00 percent has been in both the styles III and IV.

The response to question number 8 (i.e., decision as to hire machinery) show that 55.00 percent of owner-manager have been using style II and 25.00 percent style 1,13.33 percent style III and 6.67 percent style IV.

As regards to question number 9 (i.e., decision as to employ new subordinate to operate the machine) 36.67 percent of owner-managers are using style I and 35.00 percent style II. A lower percentage of responses i.e., 20.00 percent and 8.33 percent have been observed in styles III and IV respectively.

It is seen in the question number 10 (i.e., decision as to purchase a new machine) 38.33 percent of owner-managers are adopting style II, 26.67 percent, 25.00 percent 10.00 percent of owner-managers are adopting I, IV and III styles respectively.

In case of question number 11 (i.e., as to get a loan) 36.67 percent are using style I, followed by style II, (31.67 percent), III (16.67 percent) and IV (15.00 percent).

If we observe the responses for question number 12 (i.e., decision as to any other financial matter) about 40.00 percent of owner-manager are adopting style II, and 28.33 percent style I. A lower percentage of response (i.e., 16.67 and 15.00 percent) have followed style IV and III respectively.

It is seen in question number 13, (i.e., decision as to promote or punish the workers), 41.67 percent of the owner-managers are adopting style II. 37.67,13.33 and 8.33 of the respondent are adopting the styles I, IV and III respectively.

In case of question number 14, (i.e., decision to take disciplinary action against the employees) 40.00 percent of owner-managers are using style II and 35.00 percent style I. A lower percentage of responses i.e., 13.11 and 11.67 have adopted style III and IV respectively.

With regard to question number 15, (i.e., decision to assign different jobs to workers) the highest response is towards style II, ie., 36,67 percent, while the lowest is in case of style III i.e., 16.67 percent.

Of the total respondents, in case of question number 16 (i.e., decisions to remove the workers) 35.00 per cent of owner-managers are using style II while 31.67 per cent are adopting style I. An equal percentage i.e., 16.67 has been seen in both the styles III and IV.

In case of question number 17 (i.e., decision to pay compensation), 45.00 per cent are using style II followed by style I (35.00 per cent), style III (11.67 per cent) and style IV (8.33 per cent).

In view of the above discussion from the particulars furnished in the tables, it is evident that 3/4ths of the sample owner-managers are adopting autocratic style (i.e., I & II) in respect of making decisions relating to production, technical and personnel matters and 2/3rds in case of financial maters. Of the remaining I/3rd sample owner-managers 53 percent, 56 percent, 42 percent and 49 percent are adopting style III in respect of production, technical, financial and personnel matters respectively, whereas 47 percent, 44 percent, 58 percent and 51 percent are adopting style IV. None of the sample

TABLE 6

Owner-Managers Age—Leadership Styles

(N = 60)

Age Group	Styles Adopted I Number	I %to total	II Number	II %to total	III Number	III %to total	IV Number	IV %to total	V Number	V %to total	Total
20-25	26	28.89	48	53.33	10	11.11	6	6.67	—	—	90
25-30	48	21.92	93	42.47	60	27.39	18	8.29	—	—	219
30-35	101	44.69	60	27.39	35	15.49	30	13.27	—	—	226
35-40	13	29.54	11	25.00	11	25.00	9	20.45	—	—	44
40-45	4	23.53	8	47.06	2	11.76	3	17.65	—	—	17
45-50	8	23.53	13	38.24	4	11.76	9	26.47	—	—	34
50-55	12	13.64	34	38.64	13	14.77	29	32.95	—	—	88
55-60	10	32.25	11	35.48	2	6.45	18	25.80	—	—	31
60-65	40	28.78	66	47.48	18	12.95	15	10.79	—	—	139
65-70	—	—	—	—	—	—	—	—	—	—	—
70-75	20	15.15	90	68.18	9	6.82	13	9.85	—	—	132
	272	26.67	428	41.96	170	16.67	150	14.71	—	—	1020

Source: Field Survey.

owner-managers are adopting participative approaches even though there is a possibility of this approach being adopted by the owner-managers in respect of atleast in technical matters.

Further, it is thought that the leadership styles of owner-managers vary with their demographic characteristics like age, education, experience and family background and this aspect is discussed in the succeeding paragraphs. Also an attempt is made to find out whether there is any correlation between age, education experience and family background and leadership styles adopted by sample owner-mangers.

Age and leadership styles of owner-managers: The following tables exhibits different age group of owner-managers and their style of behaviour in all organizational decision situation.

Table above percents number of times a particular style is used in terms of percentages among different age-group of owner-managers. The highest percentage of times is used in case of style II by owner-managers who fall between 70-75 years age group and the same style being used by those owner-managers who fall between 20-25 years ago group. The middle aged owner-managers, though they are following style II, still they are using lesser percentage of times than those extreme younger and extreme older age group.

Style III is adopted by owner-managers coming under the age group of 25-30 constituting 27.39 percentage of times being the highest one. The same style is used by the age-group of 35-40 for 25.00 percent of times. This indicates that younger and old aged owner-managers are using style II while the middle aged group of owner-managers are using the same at a lesser percentage of times. Style IV has not been adopted either by too younger (i.e., 20-25 age group) or too old owner-managers (i.e. 70-75 age group). Also it can be seen that middle-aged owner-managers though they are

TABLE 7

Owner-Managers Education and Styles

(N = 60)

Level of Education	Styles Adopted										Total
	I		II		III		IV		V		
	Number	%to total	Number	%to total	Number	%to total	Number	%to total	Number	%to total	
S.S.C.	120	3093	180	46.39	60	15.46	28	7.26	—	—	388
Intermediate	71	35.51	48	23.76	47	23.27	36	17.82	—	—	202
Graduation	66	31.13	80	37.74	24	11.32	42	19.81	—	—	212
Technical	37	45.12	31	37.80	10	12.19	4	4.88	—	—	82
	294	33.26	339	38.35	141	15.95	110	12.44	—	—	884

Source: Field Survey.

adopting style I, II, III, style IV is being used by them for a lesser number of times. Style V is not being used by any one of the owner-managers in any age group.

Co-efficient of correlations are calculated between age and the number of times the styles is used by the samples owner-managers while making decisions relating to matters of production, technical, financial and personnel. The results are furnished in the table below:

TABLE 8

Age-Related to Owner-Managers-Leadership Styles

(N = 60)

Style	*Decisions Concerned with Production*	*Decisions Concerned with Technical*	*Decisions Concerned with Finance*	*Decisions concerned with Personnel*	*Styles in all Situations*
I	-0.6549	-0.5544	-0.5932	-0.5415	-0.5425
II	-0.7271	-0.8037	-0.7181	-0.7178	-0.7389
III	-0.6102	-0.5386	0.7629	-0.7596	-0.7243
IV	-0.5341	-0.7379	-0.7474	-0.8207	-0.8600
V	—	—	—	—	—

Source: Field Survey.

From the table above, it is evident that there is a negative relationship between age and leadership styles which implies that as the age decreases the adoption of style I, II, III and IV are increasing. This means that younger managers are adopting these styles in large number of times.

Also it is evident from the table above that in case of production and technical matters style II is being used comparatively larger number of times by younger managers. Hence, this discussion permits to conclude that younger managers have sound knowledge in production and technical matters and because of this they are not believing their workers in these matters. But the maximum correlation in technical and personnel matters reveal that there is high negative association between age and leadership styles. In case of financial and personnel matters style IV is being used dominant by younger owner-managers.

Education and Leadership Styles of Owner-Managers

As the civilization advances the day-to-day socio-economic and political set up in India has been changing accordingly. Prior to 1960 many shall scale industries in India were managed by uneducated or lowly educated entrepreneurs but later on professionalization of the management was introduced into this sector now most of these industries are held by managers of lower education. With the result the style of decision-making of owner-mangers will very with their level of education. Hence, it is felt here to examine how the leadership styles of owner-managers vary with their educational background. Particulars of the study in this respect are furnished in the table below:

It is obvious from the table above that style II is used by large number of owner-managers (38.35 mean percentage of times) followed style I (33.26 mean percentage of times), style III (15.95 mean percentages of times) and style IV (12.44 mean percentage of times.) On observation of the styles education-wise, it is found that better educated owner-managers are more flexible in using styles rather than lower educated. The more frequently used styles, irrespective of level of education are style II, I and III. Style V is not being use by any owner-manager at any education level.

Co-efficient of correlations are calculate by taking the number of years spent by the sample owner-managers on education and their styles in order to examine how the

TABLE 9

Managerial Experience and Leadership Style

(N = 60)

Years of Experience	Styles Adopted										Total
	I		II		III		IV		V		
	Number	%to total	Number	%to total	Number	%to total	Number	%to total	Number	%to total	
0-5	20	14.59	90	65.69	15	10.95	12	8.76	—	—	137
5-10	95	24.36	120	30.77	98	25.13	77	19.74	—	—	390
10-15	59	23.32	13.1	51.79	27	10.67	36	14.23	-	-	253
15-20	10	11.76	62	72.94	7	8.24	6	7.06	—	—	85
20-25	13	19.12	47	69.12	3	4.41	5	7.35	—	—	68
25-30	34	39.08	26	29.88	10	11.49	17	19.54	—	—	87
	231	22.65	476	46.76	160	15.69	153	15.00	—	—	1020

Source: Field Survey.

educational levels are correlated to the adoption of particular leadership style. The particulars in this respect are furnished in the table below:

TABLE 10

Relation of Education and Leadership Styles

(N = 60)

Style	*Decisions Concerned with Production*	*Decisions Concerned with Technical*	*Decisions Concerned with Finance*	*Decisions concerned with Personnel*	*Styles in all Situations*
I	-0.8272	-0.8731	+ 0.8272	-0.8295	-0.9795
II	+0.9428	+ 0.9285	+0.9345	-0.8782	+0.9282
III	+0.8126	+ 0.9634	+0.7388	+0.9036	+0.9393
IV	-0.5581	+0.9268	+0.8455	-0.6755	+0.6729
V	—	—	—	—	—

Source: Field Survey.

It is found from the correlated values that style I and IV are used particularly with regard to production an technical matters by low educated while style II and III are used more frequently by the higher educated particularly with regard to production, technical and financial matters. With regard to personnel matters style I and II are adopted by lower educated while III and IV by higher educated owner-managers.

On the whole it is seen that the lower educated favoured style I and IV while highly educated towards style II and III. But variations have been found in all the situations.

It can be concluded that education is having some correlation (i.e., positive or negative) with that of leadership styles. But in more cases it is found that education is positively correlated to the styles of leadership.

TABLE 11

Family Background of Owner-Managers and Their Leadership Styles

(N = 60)

Family Background	*Styles Adopted*										*Total*
	I		*II*		*III*		*IV*		*V*		
	Number	*%to total*	*Number*	*%to total*	*Number*	*%to total*	*Number*	*%to total*	*Number*	*%to total*	
S.S.C.	120	3093	180	46.39	60	15.46	28	7.26	—	—	388
Agriculture	40	33.61	27	22.69	33	27.73	19	15.97	—	—	119
Business	173	27.68	272	43.52	107	17.12	73	11.68	—	—	625
Profession	49	17.75	156	56.52	28	10.14	43	15.58	—	—	276
	262	25.69	455	44.61	168	16.47	135	13.23	—	—	1020

Source: Field Survey.

Experience and Leadership Styles

The table below incorporates the result of the years of experience of owner-managers in selected units and their leadership styles.

The results in the table above indicate that irrespective of the number of years experience most of the owner-managers have used style II followed style I, III and IV. But in case style IV, the less experienced (i.e., 5-10 years) and little experienced (i.e. 10-15 years) owner-managers used in more number of times than more experienced. Looking at the average it can be said that on an average less experienced are more flexible in using their leadership styles than the experienced.

The relationship between number of years of experience of the sample owner-managers and the number of times the styles adopted by them is examined by calculating co-efficient of correlation. The resultant figures are shown in the table below :

TABLE 12

Relationship of Experience of Owner-Managers Styles Adopted

(N = 60)

Style	*Decisions Concerned with Production*	*Decisions Concerned with Technical*	*Decisions Concerned with Finance*	*Decisions Concerned with personnel*	*Style in all situations*
I	-0.6549	-0.6099	+0.5013	+0.4793	-0.5461
II	+0.5678	+0.5272	-0.4818	+0.6200	-0.2887
III	-0.4316	+0.3533	-0.5429	+0.4959	-0.4595
IV	+0.3337	-0.3745	+0.3952	-0.3272	+0.2584
V	—	—	—	—	—

Field Survey.

The table above reveals that increase in experience is leading to decreases in using the styles I, II and III and decrease in experience is leading to increasing the democratic view i.e., style IV. In other words, these co-efficient of correlation figures suggest that owner-managers who had put in more number of years of experience are using the democratic style.

Family Background and Leadership Styles

Behaviour of a man is usually influenced by many factors like economic, social, ethical and moral values and such other sociological factors. However, among all the sociological factors the family background is one of the important factors that is to be considered while assessing one's own behaviour.

In Indian situations, especially in small scale industry most of the entrepreneurs hail from agricultured families. The style of a person who hails from business background is certainly differs to that of those from agriculture and profession. In the table that follows, it is examined how different owner-managers with different family backgrounds are following different leadership styles.

Style II is used by the agricultured family background owner-managers for 22.69 percent of times. The same style is used to the extent of 43.52 percent of times by business family background managers but the highest percentage of times the same style is used by the professional family background managers i.e., 56.52 percentage of times. Style IV is also used for 15.58 percent times by professional family background owner-managers. Hence professional family background owner-managers are more autocratic than other managers. In all the situations more frequently used style is II followed by style I and the least being style IV. The style V is not being used by any owner-manager.

In addition to finding out the family background and leadership styles, it is also examined here how these styles are correlated with their family background. Since it is not possible to correlate qualitative variables like family background with quantitative variables like responses to various styles, it is studied by taking owner-manager's education with family background and their style of behaviour. The table below shows the results.

TABLE 13

Relationship between Education with Family Background of Owner-Managers and Leadership Styles they Adopt

(N = 60)

Education with Family Background	*Styles*	*Co-efficient of Correlation*	*'t' Value*
Agriculture	I	+0.5768	0.37
	II	+0.8669	2.23
	III	+0.1685	1.24
	IV	+0.1820	1.20
	V	—	—
Business	I	-0.4936	3.56
	II	+0.3763	0.49
	III	-0.4213	3.27
	IV	-0.5026	3.60
Profession	I	+0.5979	0.42
	II	+0.7406	1.32
	III	+0.4521	0.21
	IV	+0.4076	0.41
	V	—	—

Source: Field Survey.

In the table above the correlations calculated between owner-managers' education with agriculture background and leadership styles they adopt show positive relationship. This implies that more educated owner-managers with agricultured family background are adopting style II and I.

Leadership styles and education with business background

owner-managers are negatively correlated, but style it is positively related. But the 't' tests show that these correlations have been found statistically significant.

The results show that style II has more correlation with education profession background owner-managers though not significant at 0.05 level. This means that educated with professional family background owner-managers are adopting the styles II and I.

Thus, the discussion above permits to conclude that leadership styles of owner-managers vary with the type of decision and demographic variables. Hence, the formulated hypothesis viz., leadership styles of owner-managers will vary with the type of decision, education, age, experience, and family background is accepted.

7

PRACTICE OF LEADERSHIP THEORY IN EEPC, ETHIOPIA

The Ethiopian Electric Power Corporation, as it is the big organization, it has a number of divisions, departments, sections and subunits. It will also have numerous numbers of groups, and committees at different levels, and at different districts in the country.

It is clear that different leadership styles and behaviours will be observed at the different levels of the corporation and also the same levels. And all these differences of leadership behaviours are also be resulted because of the above-mentioned factors.

Therefore, the purpose of this paper is just to describe or explain, rather than to recommend on the frequent and major leadership styles currently practiced in the corporation in the Head Office, North District, and East Districts of Addis Ababa.

Statement of the Problem

There are frequent conflicts that arise between the workers and the leaders of the corporation. Prior studies found out the majority of the conflicts were because workers were not involved in decision-making and the leaders of the corporation were practicing mostly autocratic leadership style. In my first-degree paper, which entitled *Conflict Management and Resolution Practices of the Ethiopian Electric Power Corporation*

(July 2000), I found out lack of communication and in ability of the leaders in effectively leading their group members especially the field workers the major sources of the conflicts that arise between the subordinates and leaders.

Subordinates responses. For the question "what are the main reasons for conflicts to occur? 15.96% of the options was suggested as the main source of conflict that was idea differences in achieving common goals or benefits. Nearly equally 14.89% of the given options was the second source of conflict which was lack of communication between the workers and the management (leaders). The third source of conflict was when one body tries to become superior on another body, which was 10.64% of the given options. The fourth reason suggested was when the management decided or tried to decide or tried to decide on issues that affect workers without consulting them. This was 7.45% of the given sources of conflicts. Of the given choices or sources of conflicts only 55.32% were chosen and the rest 44.68% were undersigned.

Leaders Responses

For the same question above, the first source of conflict which was 22.81% was because of lack of workers participation, i.e., when the management try to decide on issues that affect workers without consulting them. This could be a reason for the labour management conflict as shown on the response of item 10 Table 6 choice "E". Problems of communication or lack of communication and ignorance of workers' ideas by the leaders was the second main reason (19.30% of the choices) for the source of conflict. Power absurd by leaders toward subordinates, which was 17.54% of the choices, was the third source of conflict. The fourth source of conflict was competition between two bodies to become superior on another body. The rest choices were chosen equally. Of the given options 93% of them were responded.

The above finding is my hypothesis to conduct the study of the leadership style currently practiced by the majority of the leaders of the Ethiopian Electric Power Corporation.

Objectives of the Study

The objectives of the study are to :

1. Show whether the personality traits of the leaders is influential in leadership and the EEPCO workers motivation and productivity
2. Identify the major leadership behaviours that are currently practiced by the EEPCO leaders.
3. Indicate the leadership styles that would be effective if they were applied by the leaders of the EEPCO, especially field leaders working at supervisory level.

Delimitation of the Study

To make it manageable, the study is confined to the East, and the North Districts, and the Head Office of the EEPCO. The research is intended just to identify the different leadership styles/leadership behaviours and personality traits of the leaders/and the effectiveness of the leadership styles that are currently used by the leaders of the EEPCO and to check whether the personality traits of the leaders have contributions on the effectiveness of the leaders of the Corporation.

Importance of the Study

Generally, the study will allow managers, owners and workers of the Corporation and similar organizations in Ethiopia to understand the importance of effective leadership in the productivity of the workers. The study will also try to show the ways how the personnel of EEPCO (at the leadership level) can improve their leadership styles in motivating their subordinates and improving the productivity of their workers.

Limitation of the Study

Although this study could have embraced as many data as possible, because of time and financial constraints it focused only on restricted sample of subordinates (workers) and leaders (managers) who are working in the Head Office, the North and the East districts of the Addis Ababa Ethiopian Electric Power Corporation. There was also a problem to get willingness to respond (fill) the questionnaires items from certain leaders who were important for the study.

Data Treatment and Interpretation: The Data

The primary data were collected from workers employed in EEPCO of Addis Ababa of 2 (two) selected districts, which are the eastern and northern, and the head office of EEPCO. Further the primary data were also collected from the responsible managers, leaders, supervisors and bosses who are working at leadership position in the two districts and the head office.

The Research Methodology Method: Survey Study

Subject

The sample population of the study are expected to be 70 (Seventy) employees working in the two districts and the head office of EEPCO of A.A. Care will be given such that there will be nearly an equal proportion of employees from the two districts. In addition, questionnaires will be distributed to all responsible or the authorized managers, leaders and technical supervisors who are expected to be 30.

EEPCO, as it is a big organization and the only distributor or supplier of electronic power for the country, has large number of workers. The total number of workers or employees at this time is expected to be 8967. The total number of workers in the east and north districts of Addis Ababa, are 449 and 451, respectively, which can be seen from the following table.

Throughout the tables of this paper the following terms, have been used:

HO Stands for Head Office of EEPCO

ND Stands for North district of the Addis Ababa EEPCO and

ED Stands for East District of the Addis Ababa EPCO.

Number of Employees in EEPCO Ethiopia

Employees	*No.*
Head Office of EEPCO (HO) & other Zones	8067
EEPCO (ND)	451
East District of the A. A/EEPCO (ED)	449
Grand Total	8967

Research Design

Two types of questionnaires were prepared and distributed to the employees of EEPCO, which were working in the Head Office, the North district and the East district of Addis Ababa.

The first questionnaire was prepared and distributed to the ordinary workers or subordinates who did not belong to the top, the middle, or the bottom management levels. Foremen, electromechanical persons, technicians, line and technical workers and other staff filled this questionnaire. To make the discussion easy, a common name, SUBORDINATES, will be used for these groups of employees.

To compare and contrast the responses of the sample population, a similar questionnaire was prepared and distributed to the employees who were working in leadership positions. For the same reason above, a common name, LEADERS will be used to designate top and middle managers, superintendents, and technical supervisors.

As can be seen from the Appendix, most of the questions in the two type of questionnaires were similar in order to obtain more data or information and compare the corresponding views, suggestions, attitudes, and beliefs of the two groups.

TABLE 1

Number of Share Subordinates in EEPCO

			HO	*ND*	*ED*	*Total*
Distributed		No.	12	35	35	82
Collected	Technical Workers	No.	—	13	15	28
	Office Workers	No.	9	17	9	35
	Total	No.	9	30	24	63
		%	14.27	47.62	38.10	100

TABLE 2

Shares the Number of Leaders in EEPCO

		HO	*ND*	*ED*	*Total*
Distributed	Na	12	14	13	39
Collected	No.	5	10	7	22
	%	22.72	45.45	31.82	100

From the for going It can be seen that a total of 82 questionnaires were distributed to subordinates in the had office, the North District, (MD) and East (ED) respectively.

Similarly a total of 39 questionnaires were distributed almost evenly to the leaders of the head office (HO), the north district (ND) and the east district (ED) of Addis Ababa However, only 22 questionnaires of the total distributed questionnaires were appropriately filled and collected.

TABLE 3

The Sex, Age and Qualification of Subordinates

Nos.	*Item*	*Description*	*No.*	*No*	*ED*	*Total*	
			No.	*No.*	*No.*	*No.*	*%*
1.	Sex	Males	5	23	18	46	73.02
		Females	4	7	5	16	25.40
		Undesignated	—	—	1	1	1.59
		Total	9	30	24	63	100
2.	Age	21-30 yrs	4	6	2	12	19.05
		31-40 yrs	4	13	12	29	46.03
		Above 40 yrs	—	8	6	14	22.22
		Undesignated	1	3	4	8	12.70
		Total	9	30	24	63	100
		Primary Education	1	5	4	10	15.87
		Secondary Ed.	1	5	8	14	22.22
		Diploma (12+2)	5	16	11	32	50.79
3.	Qualif-	12+3	—	2	*	2	6.67
	ication	Degree	1	21	1	3	4.76
		Above Degree	—	—	—	—	—
		Undersigned	1	1	—	2	3.17
		Total	9	30	24	63	100

TABLE 4

Number of Leaders

Nos.	*Item*	*Description*	*No.*	*No*	*ED*	*Total*	
			No.	*No.*	*No.*	*No.*	*%*
1.	Sex	Males	5	9	7	21	65.45
		Females	—	—	—	—	4
		Undesignated	—	1	—	1	4.55
		Total	5	10	7	22	100

contd....

Nos.	*Item*	*Description*	*No.*	*No*	*ED*	*Total*	
			No.	*No.*	*No.*	*No.*	*%*
2.	Age	21-30 yrs	—	1	—	1	4.55
		31-40 yrs	2	4	2	8	36.36
		Above 40 yrs	3	5	4	12	54.55
		Undesignated	—	—	1	1	4.55
		Total	5	10	7	22	100
3.	Qualifi-cation	Primary Education	—	—	—	—	—
		Secondary Ed.	—	4	—	4	18.18
		Diploma (12+2)	2	5	5	12	54.55
		12+3	—	1	1	2	9.09
		—	—	—	—	—	—
		Above Degree	—	—	—	—	—
		Undersigned	—	—	1	1	4.55
		Total	5	10	7	22	100

Source: questionnaire.

Analysis and Discussion of the EEPCO Leaders Responses

Leaders questionnaires which were filled by the leaders of EEPCO consists of two parts (Please see the items at the end of the paper):

Part I. The questions in this part were designed based on the Blake and Mouton Management Grid Theory. The responses of the leaders were also summarized and analyzed using the Mathematical Analysis and Graphical presentation of the Blake and Mouton. Based on the average calculations, the leaders' opinions about their leadership style or practice were located in the management grid.

Since the leaders assessed themselves or told about their leadership style or might suggested on what they believe, it can be difficult to check/verify the reliability or the dependability of their responses. Therefore, additional, and specific crosschecking questions or items were also be included in the second part of the questionnaire.

For comparison purpose, the subordinates' response in the second questionnaire (the subordinates questionnaires) will also be analyzed about the leadership styles of their leaders.

Each leader's responses for question numbers I, 4, 6,.9, 10, 12, 14, 16 and 17 were added. The sum of these questions is multiplied by 0.2 in order to find the point of the leader in the vertical axis (Concern for people). The result of each of leader, then, added up and divided by the total number of the respondents to locate the average number of the leaders' position in the vertical axis.

Therefore, Concern for People (the average position on the axis) is:

$$\frac{\text{Position on the vertical axis}}{\text{Total number of leaders}} = \frac{136.4}{22} = 6.2$$

Similarly, the leaders' position on the horizontal axis (Concern for Production/Task) is calculated as.

$$\frac{\text{On the horizontal axis}}{\text{Total number of leaders}} = \frac{132}{22} = 6.2$$

Then, the drawing of the results is made on the management grid. The score (line) of 6.2 in the PEOPLE section and the score (line) of 6 in the TASK section intersected in the management grid. The gauge where the two lines interest shows the average leadership style of the EEPCO leaders—which is team leader (See the management grid).

It can be inferred that the average number of leaders believes that they are at the (9,9) quarter of the management

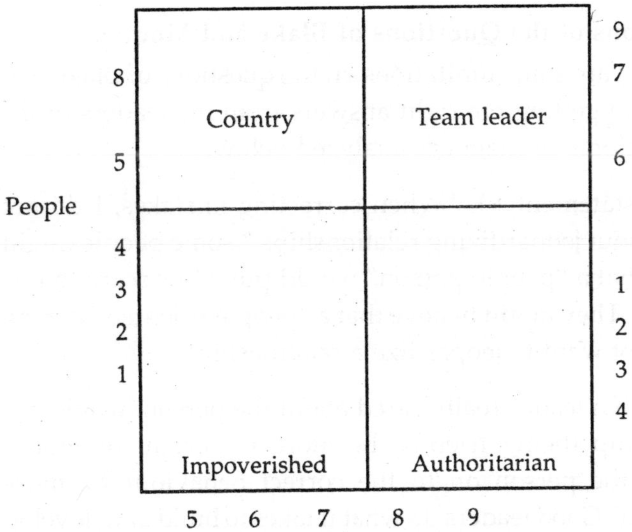

grid. In other words, their self-assessment reflected that they considered themselves, as they were 'team leaders.'

It can be inferred that the average number of leaders believes that they are at the (9,9) quarter of the management grid. In other words, their self-assessment reflected that they considered themselves, as they were 'team leaders.'

However, on the other hand, their subordinates evaluated and described them as they were and authorization leaders or they located them as they were in the (9, I) quarter of the management grid.

The leadership behaviour demonstrates two quite different results as it was differently evaluated by the leaders themselves and the subordinates, team leadership style and authoritarian leadership styles, respectively.

Based on the Management Grid Theory of Blake and Mouton, the (9,9) or team management is a desirable and meaningful leadership.

Limitations of the Questions of Blake and Mouton

There are some limitations on the questions of Blake and Mouton in getting the right answers from the leaders of the EEPCO. Some of them are analyzed below.

For statement 10- "When correcting mistakes, I do not worry about jeopardizing relationships," some people might believe that a "people-person" would put a low score to this question. They might believe that a "people-oriented" person would not want to jeopardize a relationship.

But, if a leader really cared about the person, would the relationship (being friends) be more important or would guiding the person on to the correct behaviour be more important? Good leaders do what it takes to build and develop the people around them. The "relationship" is not what makes them tick. .guiding others onto greatness is what a "people" leader is all about.

This question helps to separate the "country club leaders" who want to be friends with everyone; the "impoverished leaders" who are afraid they might make waves; and the real "people leaders" who are more concerned with coaching others so that they benefit the team. That is, if the leader lets one of her peers continue with the incorrect behaviour, does this help or hinder the other members of the team? It is best not to picture a "people" leader as a friend, but as a person who concerned with the growth and welfare of others.

Instead of presenting a manager with a dilemma of choosing one or other alternative, it shows how a leader can simultaneously maximize both production oriented methods and those that are people oriented.

The Self-Assessment

Can people assess themselves? A perfect score is a nine in both categories of People and Tasks The leaders gave a perfect score or close to it for themselves, they were being too easy on themselves-but not true on their leadership evaluations by their subordinates.

Reliability and Validity

Since this study is not a detailed study about leaders behaviour, it has not been formally checked for reliability and validity. However, since I have had a lot of feedback from various group leaders, other group leaders/supervisors, and various sources, I feel that it is fairly accurate.

Part II. The Management Grid could show us the pattern of or might give us a clue about the leadership behaviour that is currently used by the Ethiopian Electric Power Corporation leaders But it is limited to the emphasis given on each of the two dimensions- Task and People. This part includes questions that would help to find out the specific leaders' traits and a better concrete result about the leadership behaviours of the personnel of EEPCO.

Because of the inclusion of detailed questions, a summary of the analysis is made as follows.

Most of the leaders consult their subordinates on matters that involve only their actual work matters. Most of the responses reveal that the leaders were making most of the decisions. But there were also certain leaders that could give their subordinates the freedom to participate in making decision-making. This shows that different leadership behaviours were observed in the corporation.

Most of the leaders believe that participating in social activities with their subordinates would result close relationship and this would cause the subordinates not to accept orders and instructions.

Allowing subordinates to have complete freedom in their work area almost completely rejected by the leaders. This was because, leaders believe most of the workers dislike to work. Different factors could be mentioned for that they were requiring close control at work places.

As per the leaders' responses, and also they believe the workers were not skilled to take their own judgment at work. Allowing them to make their own judgment would result to wrong decisions or actions.

Most of the leaders believe that they would apply the rules and the regulations of the, corporation even if they would completely disagree with the rule and even if the particular situation forces them to bypass it.

All the workers were not equally loyal and most of them refuse to take responsibility because they have no confidence on what they were going to work. Therefore, the leaders preferred to take actions by themselves with little involvement or delegation of authority to their subordinates.

Most of the leaders gave more emphasis to the production or task than to their followers. Giving high concern for people would result works to be ignored and productivity declined, as most of the leaders believe.

It can be compared the self-assessment of the leaders questions in pan one and in the part one an in the part two investigative questions show differences in the leaders responses. The leaders' responses in part one shows that as the leaders give emphasis both to the production and people. In pan two questions, the leaders' response about the different leadership behaviours reveal that as most of the leaders were authoritarian leaders, located in the Blake and Mouton Management Grid - (9,1).

Analysis and Discussion of the Responses of Subordinates' Questionnaires

Like the "Leadership Questionnaire" the questionnaires distributed to and collected from the subordinates include two parts:

Part I - Questions in this part were designed in order to collect the subordinates perception, opinion and evaluation of their leaders and whether the personal traits of the leaders have influence on their productivity and satisfaction.

Most of the subordinates of the EEPCO believe that some personal traits of leaders have influences on the effectiveness of leaders. According to their believe, the personal traits that have influences on the effectiveness of a leader include age, appearance, academic achievement, judgment ability.

Surprisingly, most of the subordinated inversely correlated the leadership effectiveness and the age of leaders. They responded, as young leaders were more effective than their older counterparts. This might also be associated with the level of education. Most of the young leaders are educated. Most of the olden people became leaders only because of seniority. In addition, the young leaders are highly motivated than the older leaders, and they are initiated to take responsibility and challenging works.

Part III Here, the questions/items were designed to look at the actual leadership practices of their leaders and to look at how the subordinates evaluate their leadership behaviour. Two questionnaires were designed and distributed to the leaders and the subordinates of EEPCO so that comparisons can be made between the two.

Both the leaders and the subordinates gave a similar answer in that most of the leaders of EEPCO were strict about observing the rules and the regulations of the corporation. The leaders gave more emphasis on the amount of work done by the subordinates.

According to the majority responses of the subordinates, supervisors were usually give instructions and orders about what work would be done and how to be done. One-way communication was mostly practiced in the corporation.

No subordinate responded his or her supervisor was concerned about her personal and family problems. Minority of the subordinates responded that their supervisors trust them. There were situations or matters their supervisors depend on them.

Limited number of respondents were treated fairly by their supervisors. Most of the subordinates responded their supervisors gave partial treatment for those subordinates who close them and had informal relationships. This would have influenced their motivation to work with the partially treated workers and their supervisors in harmony.

Most of the leaders did not delegate authority to their subordinates and therefore, the subordinates refused to take responsibility in doing their work.

Summarizing the majority of the subordinates' responses about their immediate supervisors leadership styles/ behaviours and personality traits, the following leadership behaviours were frequently practiced by the Ethiopian Electric Power Corporation leaders:

- make most decisions by themselves without consulting their subordinates
- avoid off-the-job social contacts with employees but give special treatments for those subordinates who close them. They do not help their subordinates in solving their family and personal problems

- do not allow their subordinates complete freedom in their work and to use their own judgment in solving problems
- encourage the use of strict procedures and rules. They require subordinates or group members to follow the corporations rules and regulations
- decide on what will be done and how it will be done
- mostly do the majority of the daily work planning (specially at the supervisory and superintendents level for the field works) and call upon their subordinates to execute what they had planned
- believe in a close supervision system, and feel that display of authority will frighten their subordinates into increased productivity
- of higher management level try to build a happy and harmonious work force among their followers and avoid the use of power to get a job done
- give high concern for production rather than for people
- rarely promote an understanding of problems and a sharing of information, thoughts and ideas.
- personality traits have contributions on the subordinates productivity and satisfaction or motivation.

QUESTIONNAIRE FOR THE PERSONNEL OF THE ETHOPIAN ELECTRIC POWER CORPORATION AT THE LEADERSHIP LEVEL

Part I : Below is a list of statements about leadership behaviour. Please read each one carefully, then, using the following scale, decide the extent to which it actually applies to you. For best results, answer as truthfully as possible.

Never		Sometimes		Always	
0	1	2	3	4	5

1. I encourage my team to participate when it comes decision-making time and I try to implement their ideas and suggestions.
2. Nothing is more important than accomplishing a goal or task.
3. I closely monitor the schedule to ensure a task or project will be completed in. time.
4. I enjoy coaching people on new tasks and procedures.
5. The more challenging a task is, the more I enjoy it.
6. I encourage my employees to be creative about their job.
7. When seeing a complex task through to completion, I ensure that every detail is accounted for.
8. I find it easy to carry out several complicated tasks at the same time.
9. I enjoy reading articles, books, and journals about training, leadership, and psychology; and then putting what I have read into action.
10. When-correcting mistakes, I do not worry about jeopardizing relationships.
11. I manage my time very efficiently.
12. I enjoy explaining the intricacies and details of a complex task or project to my employees.
13. Breaking large projects in to small manageable tasks are second nature to me.
14. Nothing is more important than building a great team.

15. I enjoy analyzing problems.
16. I honor other people's boundaries.
17. Counseling my employees to improve their performance or behaviour is second nature to me.
18. I enjoy reading articles, books, and trade journals about my profession; and then plementing the new procedures I have learned.

PART II: Please answer the following statements concerning your leadership style on three point scale. Please indicate the extent to which you practice, make or believe in each of I hi' given statements. A=ALWAYS, B=OFTEN, C=OCCASIONALLY, D=SELDOM, E =NEVER

1. I make most decisions without consulting subordinates.
2. I avoid off-the-job social contacts with employees.
3. I believe employees should agree with management decisions.
4. I help the subordinates in solving their family and personal problems.
5. I allow the subordinates complete freedom in their work.
6. I permit the subordinates to use their own judgment in solving problems.
7. I encourage the use of uniform procedures and rules.
8. I let some subordinates to have authority that I should keep.
9. I try to allow the group a high degree of initiative.
10. I decide what will be done and how it will be done.

11. I refuse to explain my actions.
12. I ask the subordinates or group members to follow standard rules and regulations.
13. I do the entire planning and calls upon my subordinates to execute what he has planned.
14. I believe in a close supervision system, and feel that display of authority will frighten employees into increased productivity.
15. I try to build a happy and harmonious work force among my followers.
16. I largely avoid the use of power to get a job done.
17. I believe subordinates should be supervised, guided and aided rather than threatened and commanded to work.
18. I expect loyalty and devotion, rather than accountability, from my subordinates.
19. I believe conflict is not suppressed but is resolved by discussion.
20. I give equal weight to concern for my followers and concern for production.
21. I believe subordinates should not be driven, pushed, or forced, but are requested and motivated to do a job.
22. The leader gives high concern for people and for production.
23. I delegate authority to subordinates and make them accountable for the work allocated to them.
24. I promote an understanding of problems and a sharing of information, thoughts and ideas.

QUESTIONNAIRE FOR THE WORKERS OF THE ELECTRIC POWER CORPORATION (SUBORDINATES)

Part I. Please answer the following questionnaire items about your leader's personality traits.

1. Personality traits such as age, height, appearance, intelligence, academic achievement, judgment ability, and insight are associated with effective leadership. If you agree with this statement, please write your justifications or supporting ideas.

 ____

 ____

 ____

2. Traits of a leader may be related to effectiveness in certain situations but not in others. Agree ____________Disagree ______________ Please explain your agreement or disagreement.

 ____

 ____

 ____

3. How do you evaluate your immediate superior (Is he an effective leader)? Why?

 ____

 ____

 ____

4. Which personality traits of your leader/supervisor most likely you prefer?

 ____

 ____

 ____

5. Do the personality of your leader has influenced your motivation and productivity? Yes ______ No ______ Please explain.

____

____

____

Part II. Please answer the following questions concerning your supervisor's or your superiors leadership behaviour or leadership style on the 7-point Likert scale.

1. Is your superior strict about observing rules and regulations?
2. To what extent does your superior give you instructions and orders?
3. Is your superior strict about the amount of work you done?
4. Can you talk freely with your superior about your work?
5. Is your superior concerned about your personal problems?
6. Do you think your superior trusts you?
7. Does your superior give you recognition when you do your job well?
8. When a problem arises in your workplace, does your superior ask your opinion about how to solve it?
9. Is your superior concerned about your future benefits like promotions and pay raise?
10. Does your superior treat you fairly?
11. The leader believes that his ideas should not be questioned.
12. The leader practice one-way communication. The

leader does not encourage or accept suggestions of new ideas and better ways of doing a job from his followers.

13. The leader does not encourage or accept suggestions of new ideas and better ways of doing a job from his followers.
14. The leader relives himself of responsibility and is ready to blame his subordinates if something goes wrong.
15. The leader promotes an understanding of problems and a sharing or information, thoughts, and ideas.
16. The leader delegates authority to subordinates and make them accountable for the work allocated to them.
17. The leader gives equal weight to concern for his followers and concern for production.

REFERENCES

H. Russell Johnston, *A New Conceptualization of Sources of Organizational Climate*. Addison- Wesley Publishing Company, 1977, pp. 95-103.

Davis, Keith. *Human Behaviour at Work*, New York. Mc Graw-Hill Book Company, 1981, pp. 124-125.

Dubin, Robert, *Organizational Behaviour*. Prentice Hall, 1997, pp. 66.

Vroom, V.H., *The Search for a Theory of Leadership*. Englewood Cliff, Prentice-Hall, 397.

Stogdill, R.M. *Handbook of Leadership: A Survey of Theory and Research*. New York, 1974.

James, Owens, *The Use of Leadership Theory*, Prentice-Hall Inc. 1983 pp. 42.

Nelson, Debra Land Quick, James Campbell, *Organizational Behaviour: Foundations, Realities, and Challenges*, New York, 1997, pp. 355-356.

8

SUMMARY, CONCLUSIONS AND FINDINGS

In this last chapter, it is proposed to present an overall view of the study and to discuss the implications of its findings.

Leadership is an important factor in any form of organization whether it is small or big. One of the most significant features of the leadership situation is the style or behaviour of the leaders. It became a focal point in the emergence of modern human resource management in the organizational psychology. Sixty owner-managers of small industry belonging to Nellore town, being 10 per cent of the total, are selected as sample for the present study. A Schedule has been administered for collecting the necessary data from the said owner-managers. Personal interview was also conducted in addition to this.

A select review of literature indicates that the problem of leadership has been one of the man's major concerns since the days of antiquity. Research on leadership has often been highly normative. It has tried to find the best way of leading or of developing leaders in organizations.

This complicates the research on leadership as the dimensions of leadership which are used as variables, may come to have evaluative rather descriptive or analytical. It is difficult to specify the variables because the popular Image of leadership views it has one-dimensional-the 'tough' leader or the 'authoritarian' leader. Much of the research has considered leadership behaviour as an independent variable, comparing differences in leadership behaviour with dependent variables such as group productivity and employee satisfaction. Properties and of the group thus become intervening variables. Research treating leadership as a dependent variable may be Similarly in the early seventies, leadership, 'styles' have become a topic that is very much in vogue and many interesting theories and concepts have been putforth.

Leadership is the ability to persuade others to seek objectives enthusiastically. It determined primarily by one's role behaviour, not by one's personal traits. Leaders provide both task and psychological support for their followers. They serve role models, using combination of technical, human and conceptual skills. An important activity is goal setting as explained by path-goal of leadership. Leaders also need to able to work in an environment of power and politics. Leaders apply different leadership styles. A positive, participative and considerate leader tends to be more, effective in typical situations. However, as shown by the contingency model of leadership, a more autocratic style can be successful in situations that are either very favourable or very unfavourable to a leader.

The participative type of management is not likely to be successful in India as Indian scene is different from abroad. For example, the Indian culture is highly authoritarian and also the caste system prevalent in India encourages the tendency for security and dependency. Under these circumstances, it can be said that no style of leadership is best suited. This section intends to demonstrate the leadership styles adopted by sample owner- managers assuming the owner-manager himself as leader. As explained the owner managers are asked to indicate on the leadership continuum having five different styles in relation to each seventeen decision situations included in the decision-making questionnaire and their responses are shown in the Table ? From the summarised results, it is obvious that the owner-managers of the small scale industries use various leadership styles depending upon the situations. Hence, the formulated hypothesis viz., owner- managers use different types of leadership styles depending on the situations is accepted. Further, with a view to investigate whether the leadership styles of owner-managers vary with the type of decision, details of seventeen decision situations included in the decision- making questionnaire are kept under four groups. The responses of the owner-managers are furnished in Table. Mean percentages calculated for the responses of the investigation reveal that 3/4ths of the sample owner-managers are adopting the autocratic style in respect of decisions concerned with production, technical and personnel matters whereas 2/3rds in the case of financial matters. No one of the sample owner managers is adopting participative approach even though there is a possibility of this approach being adopted by the owner-managers in respect of atleast technical matters.

An attempt is also made here to assess whether the leadership styles of owner-managers vary with their demographic characteristics like age, education, experience and family background and co-efficient of correlations are calculated and the summarized results are shown in Tables. The results of this investigation reveal that in case of production and technical matters style II is being used comparatively large number of times by many younger owner managers and thus it leads to conclude that the younger owner managers have sound knowledge in production and technical matters. But the maximum correlation in technical (-0.8037) and personnel matters (-07178) reveal that there is high negative association between age and leadership styles. Also it is found that Style IV is being used dominantly by many younger owner-managers in case of financial and personnel matters and thereby meaning that younger managers are more flexible in decision making by consulting the subordinates. On observation of the styles education wise, it is found that higher educated owner-managers are more flexible in using styles rather than lower educated. Style I, II and III are more frequently used irrespective of the level of education and style IV is not adopted by any owner-managers at any education level. Co-efficient of correlation in this aspect reveal that style I and IV are used particularly in respect of production and technical matters by low educated whereas style II and III are used more frequently by higher educated especially in matters of production, technical and finance. In case of personnel matters style I and II are adopted by lower educated whereas style III and IV by higher educated owner-managers.

Thus, the lower educated are favouring style I and II and higher educated style III and IV though, variation exists in all the situations. It is also found that in most of the cases the level of education is positively correlated to styles of leadership. The results of investigation indicate that irrespective of the number of years of experience most of the owner-managers have adopted style II followed by style I, III, and IV. Looking at the average, it can be said that less experienced are comparatively more flexible in using leadership styles. The co-efficient of correlation between the number of years of experience and the type of leadership styles used reveal that increase in experience is leading to decrease in using the styles I, II and III and decrease in experience is leading to increase in adopting style IV i.e., democratic style. In other words, the coefficient of correlation suggests that more experienced owner- managers are more democratic in their style of behaviour. As it is not possible to correlate qualitative variable such as family background with quantitative variables like responses to various styles, it is examined by combining owner-managers' education with their family background and thereby correlating it to their style of behaviour. The results of the calculated correlation reveal that those owner-managers who are educated and hailed from agriculture families are adopting style I and II as there is positive correlation in this respect. Owner-managers who are educated and hailed from professional families are also adopting comparatively style I and II large number of times. Negative correlation is noticed between leadership style and owner-managers who are educated with business background. But in case of only style II, positive correlation is evidenced. Hence, the formulated hypothesis viz., leadership styles of owner managers will vary with the type of decision, education, age, experience and family background is accepted.

In consonance with this, the sample owner-managers have been adopting different types of leadership styles to meet different situations.. The demographic variables such as age, education etc., are also having their own role in-adopting different styles of leadership by the owner-managers.

BIBLIOGRAPHY

BOOKS

1. Adir John: *Action Centered Leadership,* McGraw- Hill, U.K., 1973.
2. Abraham: *The Dynamics of Interpersonal ZALEZINK and MOMENT DAVI Behaviour,* New York, 1964.
3. Apple, White and Philip B: *Organizational Behaviour,* Englewood Cliffs, N.J. Prentice Hall, 1965.
4. Ahmad Abad: *Management-Organization Development: A Behavioural Science Approach,* Rachna Prakashan, New Delhi, 1972.
5. Ashour: *The Contingency Model,* Southern Illinois University Press, 1977.
6. Brass, B: *Leadership Psychology and Organization Behaviour,* Henper & Row, New York, 1960.
7. Bales, R.F: *Interaction Process Analysis, A Method for the Study of Small Groups,* Cambridge, 1950.
8. Blake Robert, R: *Managerial Grid,* Gulf Publishing Company Texas, 1964.
9. Barnard, I. Chester: *The Functions of the Executive,* Harvard University Press, Cambridge, London, 1968.
10. Bennis Warren and Nanus, Burt: *Leaders: The Strategies For Taking Charge,* Harper & Row, Cambridge.
11. Browne and Cohn: *The Study of Leadership,* Danville, Dip: Interstate, 1958.
12. Cartwright, D and Zander, A.F: *Group Dynamics Research,* Harper & Row, New York, 1953.

13. Chibber, M.L: *How to Be A Successful Leader,* ANA Publishing House, New Delhi, 1986.

14. Campbell, Dunnette et al.: *Managerial Behaviour, Performance and Effectiveness,* McGraw-Hill Company, New York, 1970.

15. Daniel, C. etal: *Managing Individual and Group Behaviour in Organizations,* McGraw-Hill International Book Company, Japan, 1983.

16. Danserau, F Jr., Graen, G. and Haga, W.J.: *A Vertical Dayed Linkage Approach to leadership with in formal organizations: A longitudinal Investigation of the Roll Making Progress,* Southern Illinois University Press, Carbondale, 1982.

17. D'Souza Anthony: *Leadership: A Trilogy on Leadership and Effective Management.* Better Yourself Books, Bombay, 1987.

18. Davis Keith: *Human Behaviour At Work—Organizational Behaviour,* 6th edition, Tata McGraw-Hill Publishing Company Ltd., New Delhi, 1981.

19. Davis and Luthans: *Leadership Reexamined.*

20. David, C. Mccelland: *The Achieving Society,* D. Van Nostrand Company Inc., 1961.

21. Dinning, B.W.: The Interaction of Business Studies At The Level, In H.E. (Ed) *Organization Structuring,* McGraw-Hill, London, 1971.

22. Drucker, Peter F.: *The Practice of Management,* Allied Publishers (P) Ltd., Bombay, 1965.

23. Eyre, E.C: *Mastering Basic Management,* 1st edition, Macmillan Master Services, 1982.

24. Etzionia: *Modern Organizations,* QNJ Prentice Hall, 1964.

25. Fiedlerf, E.: A Contingency Model of leadership Effectiveness, Berkowitz (ed) *Advances in Experimental Social Psychology,* Academic Press, New York, 1964.

26. Firflrt ,F.E: *A theory of Leadership Effectiveness*, McGraw Hill Book New York, 1967.

27. Fayal Henry: *General and Industrial Management,* 1st edition SIR ISAAC Pitman & Sons Ltd., 1949.

28. Filly, A.C., House: *Managerial Process* and R.J. & KEER, S. *Organizational Behaviour*, Glenview, 111. Scott, Foresman, 1976.

29. Gordent: *Group Centered Leadership,* Boston, Houghton Mifflin Company, 1955.

30. Gibbe, A: Leadership: *In the Handbook of Social Psychology*, 2nd Edition, Volume No. 4, ed, Glindy E. Aronson Reading 1969.

31. Gibb, C.A.: *Leadership Selected Readings*, Harmondsworth, Penguin Books, Middlesex 1969.

32. Gross, B.M: *What are Your Organization Objectives A General System Approach of Planning,* Human Relations, 1965.

33. Gupta, J.L.: *Leadership Styles and Power Sharing in Business Enterprises,* Himalaya Publishing House, Bombay, 1985.

34. Hollriegel Don,: *Organizational Behaviour,* West John W. Slocumn and Richard Publishing Company, 1983.

35. Hare A.P., Borgatta,: *Small Groups Studies,* In Social E.E. & Bales, R.F Group Interaction, New York,

36. Hicks G. Herbert and Gullett Ray C: *The Management of Organization*, 3rd edition, McGraw-Hill Company, New York.

37. Haimanntheo: *Professional Management Theory and Practice,* 3rd edition, Euras-Publishing House (P) Ltd., New Delhi, 19-62.

38. House and Mitchell: *Path-Goal Theory of Leadership,* 1974.

39. Hickman Craig R & Silva Michael: *Creating Tomorrow's* Organizations Today, NAL Books, New York, 1987.

40. Heiderjohn: *Tao of Leadership Aldershot,* Hunt Wildwood House, 1985.

41. Hersey Paul and Blanchard, K.H.: *Management of Organizational Behaviour utilizing Human Researches,* Printed Hall (P) Ltd., 1982.

42. Haire M, Ghisetti E.E: *Managerial Thinking,* John Wiely, and PORTER, L.W New York, 1966.

43. Huse, E.F: *Management,* West Publishing Company, New York, 1982.

44. Iyengar, K.S: *The Philosophy of Small Scale Industrial Management,* Today-Tomorrow's Printers & Publishers, 1968.

45. Jeraid G. Batchmann,: Bases of Supervisory Power: Davud G. Bowers and A Comparative Study in Five Phillip M. Marcers: *Organizational Settings,* In Arnold, S. Tannenbaum (ed), *Control in Organizations,* McGraw-Hill Book Company, New York, 1968.

46. James, L. Gibson, John M: *Organizations, Business,* Ivancewish and James A. Publications Texas, 1979. DONALLY

47. Kolas, B.C: *Introduction to Behaviour Science in Business,* Second Wieley Easter Reprint, 1978.

48. Katz, D: *Productivity, Supervision and Morale Among Rail-Road Workers,* Arbur, Michigan, Institute for Social Research, 1950.

49. Koontz O'Donell, et al: *Management,* 8th edition, McGraw-Hill International Book Company, 1984.

50. Kochan, Schmiot & Decotiis: Supervisor-Subordinates Relations: Leadership and Headship, *Human Relations,* 1975.

51. Kahn Rand Kartz, D: *Leadership Practices in Relation to Productivity and Morale in Group Dynamics, and Theory,*

2nd edition, D. Carrwright and Zander, A (Elms Ford, N.Y. Row, Paterson) 1960.

52. Kelly Joe: *Organizational Behaviour*, Revised edition, Irwin, Homewood 111., 1974.
53. Luthansfred: *Organizational Behaviour*, 4th edition, McGraw-Hill Company, New York.
54. Mescon M.H., Hammond: *The Management and Enterprise*, W.R., Byars L.L and Foerst J.R., Macmillan York, 1973.
55. McGregor Douglas: *The Human Side of Enterprise*, McGraw-Hill Book Company, New York, 1960.
56. McGregor Douglas: *The Professional Manager*, McGraw-Hill Book Company, New York, 1967.
57. Maier, N.R.F: *Problem Solving Discussions and Conferences: Leadership Methods and Skills*, McGraw-Hill Company, New York, 1963.
58. MacGregor James: *Burns in Leaderships*, Ambika Publication, New Delhi, 1978.
59. Mathur K.C: *Small Scale Industries in India, Policies, Programmes and Institutional Support-Development* Commissioner (SSI), Ministry of Industries, Govt. of India, New Delhi, 1983.
60. McFarland and Datton, E: *Management: Principles and Practices*, McGraw-Hill Company, New York, 1973.
61. Minner John B.: *Management Process: Theory, Research and Practice*, Macmillan Company, New York, 1973.
62. Micheal H. Mescon: *The Management of Enterprise*. Section-II.
63. Miyoheishinohara and Dauglas Fisher: *The Role of Small Industry in the Process of Economic Growth*. The University of Chicago. Chicago, 1968.

64. Nord, WRD (ed.): *Concepts and Controversy in Organizational Behaviour*, Santa Monica Company, 1976.
65. Perrow C: *Organizational Analysis*, Tavistock Publications, London) 1970.
66. Phillip Mason: *The Matter of Honour*, Penguin Books, Middlesex, 1974.
67. Rensis Likert: *New Patterns of Management*, McGraw-Hill Company, New York, 1961.
68. Rensis Liker: *The Human Organization*, McGraw-Hill Book Company, New York, 1961.
69. Richard M. Hoogets: *Modern Human Relations*, The Dryden Press, Hindales Illinoiss 1980.
70. Robbins. P. Stephen: *Organizational Behaviour*, 2nd edition, Prentice Hall of India (P) Ltd., New Delhi, 1985.
71. Rao V.K.R.V.: *Role of Small Scale Enterprises in Indian Economic Development*, Asian Publishing House, Bombay, 1961.
72. Stogdill, R.M: *Hand Book of Leadership*, Free Press, New York, 1974.
73. Stogdill, R.M and Coons, A.E.: *Leader Behaviour its Prescription and Measurement*, Columbus, Bureau of Business Research, Ohio-State University, 1957.
74. Schein H. Edgar: *Organizational Psychology*, Prentice-Hall of India, New Delhi, 1979.
75. Sayles Leonard R: *Leadership: What effective Managers Really Do...... And How They Do It*, McGraw-Hill, New York, 1979.
76. Sivayya, K.V. and Dass, V.B.M: *Indian Industrial Economy*, S. Chand & Company, New Delhi, 1983.
77. Scott Willam F. and Mitchell, Terencer: Organizational Theory: A Structural and Behavioural analysis, Richard D. Irwin, Home Wood, 1972.

78. Stephen, R.M and Jones H.R: *Organizational Managers,* Intext Educational Publisher, New York, 1973.

79. Tannenbaum, R. & Schmidt, W: "How to choose a Leadership Pattern," *Harvard Business Review,* 1957.

80. Tannenbaum R. & Irwing R.: Leadership and Organization, A Beha- WESCHIER and FRED MASSARIK Vioural Science Approach, and McGraw-Hill Book Company, Inc., New York, 1961.

81. Tead Ordway: *The Art of Leadership,* McGraw-Hill Book Company, New York, 1935.

82. Terry, G.R and Franklin, S.G: Principles of Management, 8th edition, All India Traveler Book Seller, New Delhi, 1984.

83. Tausyk: *Work Organizations: Major Theoretical Perspectives,* 2nd edition F.E. Peacock, 1978.

84. Vroom V: *Work and Motivation,* John Wiley & Sons, New York, 1964.

85. Vasan Desai: *Organization and Management of Small Scale Industries,* Himalaya Publishing House, Bombay, 1979.

86. Veccho, R.P: An Empirical Examination of the Validity of Fidler Model of Leadership Effectiveness, *Organizational Behaviour and Human Performance,* 1977.

87. Vroom, V.H. and Yetton, P.W: A Normative Model of Leadership V Styles, In *Readings in Managerial Psychology,* edited By H.J. Learitt and L. Pondy, 2nd edition, University, of Chicago Press, Chicago, 1973.

88. Vroom, V.H and Yetton, P.W.: *Leadership and Decision-Making,* PittsBurgh: University of Pittsburg Press, 1973.

89. Weissenburg, D and Kavanaugh, W.H: *The Independence of Initiating and Structure and Consideration, A Review of Evidence Personnel Psychology,* 1972.

90. Weisshowardm: *Subordinate Imitation of Supervisor Behaviour: The Role Modeling in Organizational Socialization Organization Behaviour and Human Performance*, 1973.
91. Walter Hill: *Leadership Styles: Rigid or Flexible*, Organization Behaviour and Human Performance, 1973.
92. Yulk, G.A: *Leadership in Organization*, Englewood Cliffs, N.J. Prentice Hall, New Delhi, 1981.
93. Zahn, G.L. and Wolf, G A: Leadership and the Art of Cycle Simulation Model of Superior-Subordinate Interaction, Organizational Behaviour and Human Performance, 1981.
94. Ramanav: Leadership Styles in Small Scale Industries - A Case Study of Anantapur District, Unpublished Thesis Submitted to Sri Krishnadevaraya University, Anantapur.

JOURNALS

1. Alberts King: Evolution of Leadership Theory, *Vikalpa*, Volume 15, No. 2, April - June, 1950.
2. Anand Ram, V.,: Management Styles in Banking, *Productivity*, Volume XXVI, 1985.
3. Beverly, M. Albanmetcalfe: Leadership: Extrapolating From Theory and Research to practical Skills Training, *Journal of Management Studies*, Volume 19, No. 3, July, 1982.
4. Bavelasalex: Leadership: Man and Function, *Administrative Science Quarterly*, Volume 4, No. 4, March, 1960.
5. Christopher Clorke Simon Pratt: Leadership's Four-Part Progress, *Management Today*, March, 1985.
6. Davis R.V. and Luthans Fred: A Social Learning Approach to Organizational Behaviour, *Academy of*

Management Review, April, 1980.

7. Dubhashi P.R: Leadership and Administration, *Indian Journal of Training and Development*, Volume 14, No.2 April -June- 1984.
8. Evans, M.G: The Effects of Supervisory Behaviour on Path-Goal Relationship Organizational Behaviour and Human Performance, Volume 5,1970.
9. Eugen Emerson Jennings: The Anatomy of Leadership, *Management Personnel Quarterly*, Volume 1, No. 1, Autumn, 1961.
10. Fredric G. Donner: *Harvard Business Review*, May-June, 1977.
11. Garaen G. Alvares: Contingency Model of Leadership and K.M., ORRIS J.B & MARTELLA J.A Effectiveness, Antecedent Evidential Results, *Psychology Bulletin*, 1970.
12. Gross Edward: Dimensions of Leadership, *Personnel Journal*, Volume 40, No. 5, October, 1961.
13. House Robert, J.: A Path-Goal of Leadership Effectiveness, *Administrative Science Quarterly*, Volume 16,1971.
14. House Robert J and Path-Goal: Theory of Leadership Terence R. Mitchell *Journal of Contemporary Business*,
15. James V. Spotts: The Problems of Leadership: A Look At Some Recent Findings of Behavioural Science Research, *Business Review*, Volume 17, June, 1964.
16. Katz Robert: Skills of An Effective Administrator, - Harvard *Business Review*, January -February 1955.
17. Korman A.K: Consideration and Initiating Structure and Organizational Criteria, A Review Personal Psychology, *A Journal of Applied Research*, XIX, No. 4, Winter, 1966.
18. Lewin K, Lippitt, R. & White R.K: Patterns of Aggressive

Behaviour in Experimentally Created, Social Climates, *Journal of Psychology*, 1939.

19. Lokhande, M.R and Singh S.N.: Leadership Patterns and Social Change, *Journal of the Council of Social Development* Volume 7, No.l, March, 1977.
20. Mann, F.C and Dent, J.: The Supervisor Member of Two Organizational Families, *Harvard Business Review*, Volume 32, No.6,1954.
21. Morse, N.C and Reimer, E.: The Experimental Change of Two Organizational Variables, *Journal of Abnormal and Social Psychology*, Volume 52, 1956.
22. Muttayab, C & Vijaya Kumar: Leadership Styles, Perused Need- Satisfaction and Subjective Job Characteristics among Scientific Personnel, *Indian Journal of Industrial Relations*, Volume 25, No.3, January, 1990.
23. Morse C. Nancy and Everett Reine: The Experimental Change of Major Organizational Variable, *Applied Social Psychology*, January, 1958.
24. Mysteomwpaul: Managers and the Hi-Hi Leaders, *Academy of Management Journal*, June, 1978.
25. Neelam Varma: A Test of Implicit Personality Theories of Leadership, *Indian Journal of Industrial Relations*, Volume 22, No.2, October, 1986.
26. Pathak, R.D: A Study of Self-Perception of Leadership Styles, Leadership Effectiveness and Job-Involvement of Bank Officers, *Prajna*, Re-printed From Volume IX, 1980.
27. Prabhakar Singh: Nurturant Task and Participative Task Leadership: The Effective Leader Behaviours For Indian Industries, *Indian Journal of Industrial Relations*, Volume 23, No.2, October, 1987.

28. Porter, L.W.: A Study of Perceived Need Satisfaction in Bottom and Middle Management Job, *Journal of Applied of Psychology*, 1961.

29. Rastogi, P.N: Essence of Leadership, *Vikalpa*, Volume 12, No. 4, October-December, 1987.

30. Strube, M.J and Garcia, J.E: *"Meta Analytic Investigation of Fiedler's Contingency Model of Leadership Effectiveness, Psychological Bulletin,"* 1981.

31. Sales, S.M: Supervisory Styles and Productivity, Review and Theory, *Personal Psychology*, 1966.

32. Sinhaj, B.P: Socio-Technological Determinants of Work Values, *Indian Journal of Industrial Relations*, 1986.

33. Sehriesheim and Kerr Barbara Karmel: Leadership: A Challenge To and Traditional Research Methods and Assumptions, *Academy of Management Review*, July, 1978.

34. Swarna Pratap & Srivastava, S.K: Leadership Styles and Effectiveness A Comparative Study, *Indian Journal of Industrial Relations*, Volume 21, No.l) July, 1985.

35. Stewart, R.: Managers and Their Job, London: Pan Books, Marples, D.L., (1967) *Studies of Managers—A Fresh Start, Journal of Management Studies.*

36. Singh, R.R and Janak Pandey: Leadership Styles Control, Strategies and Personal Consequences, *Indian Journal of Industrial Relations*, Volume 22,1 No. l, July, 1986.

37. Tannenbaum Robert: How to Choose A Leadership Pattern, Warren, H. Schmidt, H. *Harvard Business Review*, March- April, 1958.

38. Venkatapathy : Perception of Top Management Leadership Styles and Climate: A Study of Public and Private Executors, *Indian Journal of Industrial Relations*, Volume 25, No.3, January, 1990.

39. Viscount, F.M.: Leadership, *The Journal of The British Institute of Management*, Management Publications Ltd., Volume 30, No.l, January, 1962.

NEWSPAPERS

1. Singh, P.N : Improving Leadership Index Through Grid, *The Economic Times,* Volume XXV, No.241, 2nd November. 1985.
2. Ramji, S.: Adopting to the Winds of Change Small Business, *The Hindu,* Thursday, August 28, 1986.
3. Ramchandra, S.R. : Dynamics of Executive Leadership, *The Hindu,* Monday, April 30th. 1984.
4. Murthy, B.S.: Organizational Ethos and Good Leadership, *The Hindu,* Thursday, December 26th, 1985.
5. Gopinath, C: Managerial Issues in Reviewing Sick Units, *The Hindu,* Thursday June 5th, 1986.
6. Batala, S.K.: Traits of Effective Leadership, *The Hindu,* Thursday, November 6th 1986.

INDEX

M

N

O

P

R

S

T

V

W

W

●●●